SCIENCE, MEANING, & EVOLUTION

Science, Meaning, & Evolution

THE COSMOLOGY OF JACOB BOEHME

BY BASARAB NICOLESCU

Translated from the French

by Rob Baker

Parabola Books

New York

1991

SCIENCE, MEANING, AND EVOLUTION

A Parabola Book / November 1991

La Science, le sens, et l'evolution: Essai sur Jakob Boehme, suivi d'un choix de textes was originally published by Éditions du Félin, Espace Iron, 10 rue La Vacquerie, Paris, France 75011. © 1988 by Éditions du Félin.

English translation Copyright © by PARABOLA BOOKS 1991.

Parabola Books is a publishing division of The Society for the Study of Myth and Tradition, a not-for-profit organization devoted to the dissemination and exploration of materials related to myth, symbol, ritual, and art of the great religious traditions. The Society also publishes PARABOLA, *The Magazine of Myth and Tradition*.

This publication has been made possible, in part, by a grant from the New York State Council on the Arts.

ISBN 0-930407-20-2

PARABOLA BOOKS
656 Broadway
New York, NY 10012

Manufactured in the United States of America

To Michelle,
who has always helped me pass
beyond the wheel of anguish

Contents

Texts by Jacob Boehme

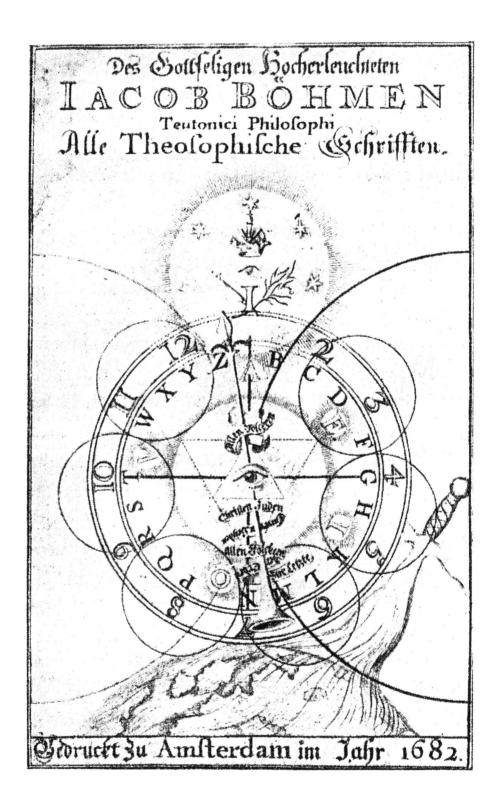

Des Gottseligen Hocherleuchteten
IACOB BÖHMEN
Teutonici Philosophi
Alle Theosophische Schrifften.

Gedruckt zu Amsterdam im Jahr 1682.

"What good will thy knowledge do thee, if thou wilt not strive and *fight* therein? It is just as if one knew of a great treasure, and would not go for it; but, though he knoweth he might have it, would rather *starve* for hunger in the *bare* knowing of it."

—Jacob Boehme, *The Aurora*

" . . . the sacred is not a stage in the history of consciousness, it is a structural element *of* that consciousness."

—Mircea Eliade, *Ordeal by Labyrinth*

Foreword

S INCE this is a book about the union of opposites and the reconciliation of contraries, it will probably appeal to two distinct types of readers. First, there will be those who suspect that modern science may be teetering on the edge of an abyss of discovery as formidable as the Copernican Revolution. To them this Foreword is addressed. Second, there are those already familiar with Jacob Boehme or with Western esotericism, who feel that their philosophic studies cannot be isolated from the scientific problems of today. Antoine Faivre's Afterword will speak to that constituency.

What common ground could possibly serve for a conversation between Basarab Nicolescu, a modern physicist, and Jacob Boehme, a Renaissance visionary? To most people science is fact, imagination is fiction, and that is the end of the matter. Yet this very split, which was opening in Boehme's century and which may begin to close in our own, is the symptom of a perilous disharmony in our inner and outer worlds. Several decades ago there was a noisy debate, opened by the British scientist C.P. (later Lord) Snow, who was also a popular novelist, concerning what he called "the Two Cultures." Snow warned that the scientific and the humanistic communities were growing further and further apart, to the degree that a member of one "culture" was not only incapable of understanding the language and interests of the other, but did not even value them. The scientists had become enmeshed in a world of technology and quantitative thinking, to which the qualitative world of arts and letters, philosophy, and religion was at best a pleasant garnish; while the humanists were quite content to be mathematically and scientifically illiterate, secure in the superiority of their pursuits to dirty jobs like engineering. Snow left his audience in no doubt about the potential danger of such a cleavage.

If there has been any improvement in the situation since those early 1960s, it is probably thanks to the scientists, and especially to physicists, many of whom have been driven by the discoveries of this century to become "metaphysicists." There is a certain hierarchy among scientists, in the sense that the principles on which one science is based serve another as materials for study. Engineers and other technicians do not need to argue about the principles handed to them by the theoretical sciences, such as biology, chemistry, and physics. Biologists, generally speaking, rely on the laws of chemistry, while chemists take for granted the principles of physics. Yet the chemists' useful models of atomic structure are fictions to the contemporary physicist. Can one go a stage further, and say that the principles taken for granted by the physicist are studied by the metaphysicist? In some circles, one might be forgiven for such talk, since at its highest and most speculative levels, physics now investigates what is beyond (*meta*) the physical world, and treats—with what surprise at its own audacity!—the very questions of being and non-being that were once reserved for philosophers.

Humanists might object to the idea of a parallel hierarchy being drawn among their own disciplines, unless they remember that Theology was traditionally regarded as reigning like a queen over the Liberal Arts, the latter being based on human investigation rather than on divine revelation. But what discipline is it that studies the principles of theology? It is a delicate question, to which a number of answers are possible. First, and least likely to be of interest today, is the denial that any discipline could exist above the "revelations" of scriptures such as the Torah, Quran, or New Testament. That is the exoteric view. Second, and more positively, there is metaphysics, the study of the principles of existence and nonexistence, including those of God. This is unbounded by the dogmas of any one religion, since its principles, if true, must be universal. Metaphysics is an esoteric study, in the sense that it concerns not the outward forms but the "inward" (*eiso*) side of religion. Basarab Nicolescu refers to one particular development of it, associated with the name of René Guénon, under the name of "Tradition." Third, there is theosophy, broadly definable as the experiential study of things divine.

The theosophical investigation of the powers behind and within the universe, which some call God or the gods, is rightly held in suspicion: history is too full of cranks and fanatics who have pretended to such intimacy. Very occasionally, however, a theosopher appears whose claims demand serious attention by those in search of wisdom. Jacob Boehme is such a one: his claim rests both on his unimpeachable personal integrity, and on the spiritual fruitfulness of his theosophic findings. Now, if Basarab Nicolescu is correct, there is a third warrant, in the applicability of Boehme's system to the problems facing modern science, and indeed modern humanity.

The reader will find in this book an admirably lucid summary of some of Boehme's findings, supplemented by primary sources from the theosopher's own writings. If fruitfulness is at issue, then this book is one of the richest fruits to grow from the Boehmian tree. Put as simply as possible, its thesis is that Boehme, through some faculty of super-sensory vision, was able to behold the principle behind the creation and evolution of the cosmos. If that were in any way true, such knowledge should definitely be of interest to contemporary science. Moreover, Boehme does not stop at explaining how the cosmos came into existence — an unsolved question, but one with which physics is at least comfortable — but continues to explain how and why it has evolved since then. In order to discuss this, he is obliged to touch on the ultimate qualities of good and evil and on their deepest roots in the divine nature. The time has come, Basarab Nicolescu suggests, for science to stop cutting itself off from such matters and concerns, as if they were any less "real" than the waves and particles to which physics has reduced our world.

Boehme's first principles are the three metaphysical forces behind the universe's existence. They begin not with God, which is the first Being, but with the *Ungrund* of Non-being (or Beyond-being) in the sight of which even the Creator and its cosmos are as nothing, yet which paradoxically gives rise to them both. Here Boehme raises to its uttermost limit the hermetic principle of polarity as the generator of existence, and also plumbs to its depths the problem of what we experience as evil. Boehme's second series of principles, seven in number, unfurl the development of the cosmos and of its creative witness, the human mind and soul, revealing the tragedy and the promise that underlie cosmic and human evolution.

In his deservedly popular work, A Brief History of Time (New York: Bantam Books, 1988), Stephen Hawking concluded with enigmatic musings on the existence or non-existence of God, in a dramatic demonstration of how physics precipitates such questions nowadays. Unfortunately the dialogue between Hawking and his readers could not proceed further, because it was couched in the language of theology, not that of metaphysics and still less of theosophy. Hawking was writing for people who, if they had any religious beliefs, were likely to have exoteric ones. Hence the question of what God is and whether it "exists" could not be treated with the requisite subtlety.

While Hawking's book began with an exposition of physics and astronomy, and ended with a theosophic question, this book begins with an exposition of Boehme the theosopher and ends with a questioning of science no less searching than the challenge Hawking offered to the theists. Yet there is perhaps more hope for the present approach, since it is founded on the principles of esotericism. Physics itself has been compelled to become "esoteric," i.e., to go beyond the nineteenth-century images of reality that are still acceptable to the majority of mankind. This compulsion has come from what one can justifiably call the visions and illuminations of Max Planck, Albert Einstein, Niels Bohr, Werner Heisenberg, et al. —all men of a distinctly metaphysical temperament. Religion, on the other hand, has declined to listen to theosophers such as Plotinus, Meister Eckhart, and Boehme, and is thus mired in exoteric stagnation. Only within a doubly esoteric framework can the two cultures be reconciled.

It is moving to witness this encounter of a sophisticated and cosmopolitan physicist with a man from the opposite end of the modern age: blunt, unschooled, and untraveled except on inward paths. Especially impressive is Nicolescu's humility in the face of the shoemaker's revelations. That it might fall to the destiny of Boehme's work to break the imaginal and moral impasse of modern science borders on the incredible. Yet within these pages, the inconceivable has actually taken place.

—Joscelyn Godwin

Translator's Note

OTH in the main section of this book about Jacob Boehme and in its appendices, we have employed the standard English translations of Boehme's own writings by John Sparrow (*The Aurora, Concerning the Three Principles of the Divine Essence,* and *Mysterium Magnum*) and John Rolleston Earle (*Six Theosophic Points, Six Mystical Points* and *Mysterium Pansophicum*), just as the standard French translations of Boehme's German original were used in the original French edition of this book.

Sparrow's translations were done in England in the mid-seventeenth century; they have a somewhat old-fashioned ring to them at times, but no other English translation has ever captured the brilliantly bombastic style of Boehme in quite the same way.

Since it is currently difficult to find any of Boehme's longer major works in English, the selections made by Basarab Nicolescu from Boehme's own texts become all the more valuable. The reader who wishes to read further in Boehme might try: *Jacob Boehme: Essential Readings,* edited and introduced by Robin Waterfield (Wellingborough, England: Crucible/Thorsons, 1989), a good selection of snippets with, unfortunately, no indication of sources or translators; *The 'Key' of Jacob Boehme,* translated by William Law (Grand Rapids, MI: Phanes Press, 1991); *The Way to Christ,* translated by John J. Stoudt (Westport, CT: Greenwood Publishing Group, 1979); and a number of shorter works, including *Six Mystical Points, Of the Supersensual Life,* and *Fundamental Statement Concerning the Earthly and Heavenly Mysteries (Mysterium Pansophicum)* (all from Holmes Publishing Group, P.O. Box 623, Edmonds, WA 98020). Most of the

Holmes editions are the John Sparrow translations, and the company intends to bring out *The Aurora, The Threefold Life of Man*, and *Forty Questions of the Soul* in the near future.

Basarab Nicolescu is eminently qualified to undertake this study of Jacob Boehme's ideas in the light of contemporary science. A leading theoretical physicist in Paris at the Centre National de Recherches Scientifique, he has also been a major force in advocating a "trans-disciplinary" approach in modern science and culture, an effort he describes as "a first step towards a dialogue between different fields of knowledge," particularly between science and traditional religious ideas. He was among sixteen thinkers from around the world who participated in a UNESCO conference called "Science and the Boundaries of Knowledge: The Prologue of Our Cultural Past" in Venice in March, 1986.

Born in Romania, he moved to Paris in 1968 and obtained his doctorate at the University of Paris. His own writings include the ground-breaking and award-winning study of elementary particle physics, *Nous, la particule et le monde* (Paris: Le Mail, 1985).

In examining Boehme's ideas in terms of contemporary physics, the author quotes extensively from a number of modern scientific studies, both popular and academic; when English editions of these books exist, we have cited the publishing information in the footnote sections at the end of each chapter, but it was not possible to check the English editions of each of these works, so some of the citings have been translated from the French (and may be at some variance with the American or British editions).

Basarab Nicolescu has graciously looked over this translation for accuracy, as has PARABOLA's founder and editorial director, D.M. Dooling. The translator also wishes to thank Joscelyn Godwin, David Appelbaum, Jean Sulzberger, and Paul Jordan-Smith for reviewing the manuscript and offering helpful suggestions.

—Rob Baker

Preface

HY WRITE about Jacob Boehme today?

Some possible misunderstandings need to be cleared up, right from the start.

Jacob Boehme (1575-1624) is a giant in Western thought and his writings have been the subject of countless able, scholarly commentaries. Fairly unknown in France outside of a small circle of specialists, Boehme at least has benefited from two critical analyses available to a wider public: *La Philosophie de Jakob Boehme* by Alexandre Koyré[1]* and *La Naissance de Dieu* by Pierre Deghaye.[2] The present book is neither a scholarly study nor a popularization of Boehme's thinking, for the author's own area of specialization is elsewhere, in the field of science. It is simply a question of presenting an entrance gate: a personal reading, offered by a modern man of culture interested in the advent of a new rationality in today's world.

Another misunderstanding, leading inevitably to such self-interested considerations as "a great mystic seen by a contemporary physicist" or "physicists and the irrational," also ought to be dispelled vigorously. First of all, Boehme is not really a mystic, but rather a representative of gnostic thought. The work of the man whom Hegel called "the foremost German philosopher"[3] and who exerted a definite influence on personalities as diverse as Newton, Novalis, Schlegel, Goethe, Fichte, or Schelling is an integral part of our culture. Thus it is normal that a physicist who is convinced that science is a part of culture, and that a dialogue between different forms

---

* *In order not to overload the text, most notes are grouped at the end of each chapter.*

of knowledge is more necessary today than ever before, should examine Boehme's work from a modern perspective.

More precisely, this book arose out of the encounter between a
passionate interest and a question.

My reading led me by chance to discover the writings of Boehme a
little more than fifteen years ago, and it was a revelation. Indeed,
Boehme has the reputation of writing in a highly obscure way, and his
language can perplex and even irritate a modern reader. But when the
framework of symbolic interpretation—the only appropriate one—is
used, Boehme's writings become crystal clear and can be read as easily
as a detective novel—a novel about everything which exists or is
conceivable: divinity, the cosmos, ourselves.

This passionate interest helped me to explore a question that I had
already formulated in my book, *Nous, la particule et le monde:*[4] how did
it happen that modern science was born in the West? Numerous works
in the tide of orientalism that sweeps over us today state that Eastern
concepts are very like those which form the basis of modern physics.
But nevertheless modern science was born here, in the West. Historical or economic arguments are not enough to answer so vast a question. An in-depth study of a way of thinking and imagining that leads
to a certain vision of the world, characteristic of a given epoch, is
indispensable for a rigorous approach to this question. In this context,
the work of Boehme seems to me an exemplary case, showing in a
typical way a whole spiritual and cultural environment that contains
the seed of modern science.

Boehme's work can lead us even further, helping us discover the
existence of a basic link between Western tradition and modern
physics. Modern science defines itself, on the whole, by its breach with
religion and Tradition, like a baby which has left its mother's womb.
But doesn't a baby, even when grown, in spite of everything retain a
link with its mother, even if the link is only genetic? In our time, the
split between science and Tradition is made absolute by proclaiming
that any coming together of the two is dangerous and illusory.[5] Excep-
tions to this bias are rare, though I could cite the important work of
Charles Morazé, *Les Origines sacrées des sciences modernes.*[6] In gathering the fruits of prolonged scholarly research, Morazé has succeeded in
identifying some structural constants, such as three-sided and four-

sided figures, which cross the boundaries between science and Tradition. But I believe it is possible to establish that the work of Boehme, examined anew as exemplary, permits us to broaden this somewhat narrow framework. We can then discover, through admittedly different methodologies, a continuity on a higher level of a true vision of the world, which is nourished by everything that historical time can bring to it.

The reader should understand that I firmly place the writings of Boehme in modernity. I share completely the opinion of Deghaye, when he affirms: "We do not make of Boehme the precursor of modern philosophy. We consider his wisdom for itself. . . . The offshoots of his teaching often concealed that wisdom. In order to rediscover Boehme, we must disengage ourselves from romantic literature and idealistic philosophy. We should especially forget Hegel."[7] But I find Deghaye more difficult to follow when he writes: "Boehme is not in the least a modern philosopher. His thought is not developed on the plane of abstract thinking."[8] Why reduce all modern philosophy to abstract thought? It is true that the label can be applied to a good deal of Western philosophy, with its strong literary tradition, which ignores the lived, the experiential aspect of life — and especially ignores science. More precisely, most philosophers either prefer to ignore science completely, conceiving of it as a group of technically operative recipes with nothing to say on the ontological plane, or they invoke it from time to time as a passing illustration. However, science today is capable of giving a new inspiration to philosophy. It cannot be reduced to abstract thinking: it is concerned essentially with Nature's resistance to our representations and to our experiences. In this sense, science represents moments of *the history of reality*. How can one conceive of a modern philosophy which ignores the history of reality?

Therefore I consider Boehme to be not a *precursor* of modern philosophy, but a modern philosopher himself. His writings are alive, like all the great texts of mankind: they nourish themselves on time and on history. It is true that his work is founded on a *lived* experience which perhaps, in its deep roots, is imagined outside of geographical space and historical time. But it offers us a vision of the double nature of Nature: a Nature which is *at once* eternal and anchored in time.

Like a modern physicist, Boehme is haunted by the idea of the invariance of the cosmic processes and by the paradoxical coexistence of unity and diversity. All is movement, in a continual creation and annihilation, in a perpetual genesis where nothing is stable and permanent. But this movement is not chaotic or anarchic; it is structured, organized by virtue of an order that is certainly complex and subtle, but nevertheless perceivable. As Boehme says to us continually, "even God is begotten by this movement, he is born not in the world but with the world."

The absence of a system of values adapted to the complexity of the modern world could lead us to the self-destruction of our own species. The formulation of a new philosophy of Nature seems to me, in this context, of immediate urgency. Jacob Boehme is among us in this quest: he is our contemporary.

NOTES

1. Alexandre Koyré, *La Philosophie de Jakob Boehme* (Paris: Vrin, 1971).
2. Pierre Deghaye, *La Naissance de Dieu ou La doctrine de Jakob Boehme* (Paris: Albin Michel, Collection *Spiritualités Vivantes*, 1985).
3. G.W.F. Hegel, "Conférences sur l'histoire de la philosophie," 1817; in *Jakob Boehme* (Paris: Albin Michel, Collection *Cahiers de l'Hermétisme*, 1977), p. 111.
4. Basarab Nicolescu, *Nous, la particule et le monde* (Paris: Le Mail, 1985).
5. Henri Atlan, *À Tort et à raison* (Paris: Seuil, 1986).
6. Charles Morazé, *Les Origines sacrées des sciences modernes* (Paris: Fayard, 1986).
7. Deghaye, p. 20.
8. *Ibid.*, p. 19.

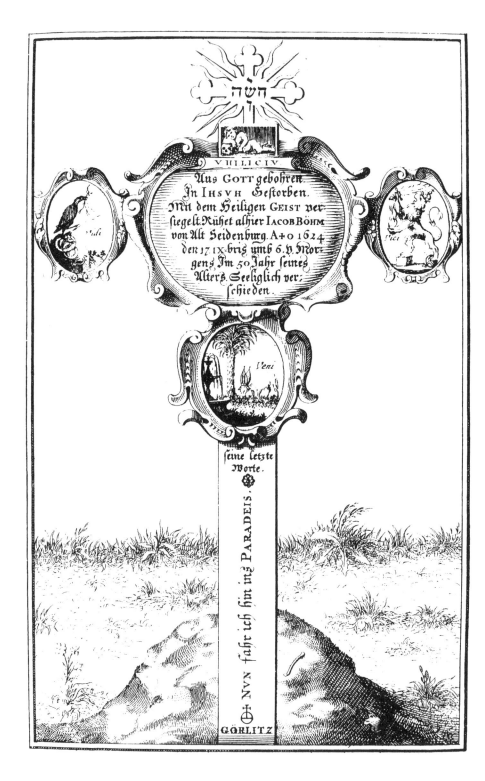

החשׁי

VIILICIV

Aus Gott gebohren.
In Ihsvh Gestorben.
Mit dem Heiligen Geist ver-
siegelt. Ruhet alhier Iacob Böhm
von Alt Seidenburg. A+o 1624
den 17 IX-bris ymb 6. H. Mor-
gens, Im 50 Jahr seines
Alterß. Seeliglich ver-
schieden.

Vidi

Vici

Veni

seine letzte
Worte.

Nvn fahr ich hin inß PARADEIS.

GÖRLITZ.

Jacob Boehme, the Man

O THOSE familiar with the writings of Jacob Boehme, what is surprising about his life is its relatively ordinary character: nothing could be further from the clichés associated with the lives of mystics or illuminati.

This resident of Görlitz, Germany, was a member of the cobblers union, married a butcher's daughter, and fathered several children. After selling his shoemaking shop, he opened a yarn store. According to Alexandre Koyré, "In 1619 and 1620 we see him in Prague dealing in woolen gloves, which he buys from the peasants of the Lusace region to resell at the market."[1] His enemy, Gregor Richter, the leading pastor of Görlitz, accused him of being a dangerous heretic, and Boehme was persecuted and even jailed for a short time. And a few days after his death, the citizens of Görlitz shattered and vandalized the cross on his tombstone. But nonetheless Boehme died a quiet death, in his own bed, after a relatively commonplace illness.

The mystery of Boehme is found elsewhere: in his experiences of "illumination." At the age of twenty-five, he had a revelation that was the basis for all his subsequent work: while gazing at the brightness of a pewter vase, he felt himself suddenly engulfed by an extraordinary flow of information about the hidden nature of things. This data was incomprehensible to him at first, and he waited twelve years to understand what had been "given" to him in that unforgettable moment. In our day, a person undergoing such an experience would immediately found a group of disciples and start giving lectures and writing best sellers. But Boehme waited twelve years, in almost total silence, in order to analyze, decipher, and explain what he had "seen" in that

moment of grace. Out of this gestation came the magnificent and
unique work, *The Aurora*.[2]

Boehme remained very discreet about his experiences of illumination, especially the first experience in 1600. But when he finally did
discuss it, the force and the sincerity of his description were both
striking and troubling. In a letter addressed in 1621 to Caspar
Lindner, the customs officer of Beuthen, he wrote: "The gate was
opened unto me, so that in one quarter of an hour I saw and knew more
than if I had been many years together at a University; at which I did
exceedingly admire, and I knew not how it happened to me; and
thereupon I turned my heart to praise God for it. For I saw and knew
the being of all Beings; . . . also the birth or eternal generation of the
holy Trinity; the descent, and original of this world."[3]

In *The Aurora*, the essential character of his vision is affirmed with
even greater clarity: "In this light my spirit suddenly saw through all,
and *in* and *by* all the creatures, even in herbs and grass it knew God,
who he is, and how he is, and what his will is: And suddenly in that
light my will was set on by a mighty *impulse*, to describe *the being of
God*. But because I could not at once apprehend the *deepest* births of
God in their *being*, and comprehend them in my *reason*, there passed
almost *twelve* years, before the exact understanding thereof was given
me. . . . So also it went with this spirit: The first fire was but a *seed*,
and not a constant lasting light: Since that time many a cold wind
blew upon it; but the will never extinguished."[4]

In spite of Boehme's discretion, it is apparent that he must have
passed through considerable inner turmoil during these twelve years
of silence, in his attempt to reconcile the richness of his experience
with the poverty of the written word to explain it. He speaks of a
"horrible abyss": "My sun was often eclipsed or *extinguished*. . . ."[5] He
writes also that ". . . . if the spirit were withdrawn from me, I could
neither know nor understand *my own writings*."[6] Boehme the cobbler
and glove merchant, responsible for the material needs of his own
family, confesses sincerely the temptation to give up: "For when I took
care for the *belly*, and to get my *living*, and resolved to *give over* this
business in hand, then the gate of heaven in my knowledge was bolted
up."[7] But he did pass through these inner trials and arrived at a
powerful point of equilibrium, where the written word did not betray

the depth of the experience: ". . . . it is laid upon me as a work which I must exercise. Therefore seeing it is my work that my spirit driveth, I will write it down for a Memorial, in such a manner as I know it in my spirit, and in such a manner as I attained to it, and I will set down no strange thing, which myself have not tried [and known], that I be not found a liar concerning myself before God."[8] How many books of philosophy would never have been written if others had followed this splendid precept of Boehme?

Boehme mistrusted all proof by logical reason that was not based on inner experience and that, going around in circles, could lead only to illusion and folly: "I *have read* the writings of very high masters, hoping to find therein the ground and true depth; but I have found nothing, but a *half dead* spirit. . . ."[9] As for his own method of writing, Boehme reveals clearly: "Thou must know that I do not suck it out from the dead or mortal *reason*, but my spirit qualifieth*, mixeth or uniteth with God, and proveth or searcheth the *Deity*, how it is in all its births and genitures. . . ."[10]

He also wrote: "There ought no historical skill and knowledge to be sought for in our writings. . . . Indeed we carry the heavenly treasure in an earthly vessel, but there must be a heavenly receptacle hidden in the earthly, else the heavenly treasure is not comprised nor held. None should think or desire to find the lily of the heavenly bud with deep searching and studying, if he not be entered by earnest repentance in the New Birth, so that it be grown in himself; for else it is but a history, where his mind never findeth the ground. . . ."[11]

An inattentive reader might conclude that Boehme is an adversary of reason. At a recent colloquium organized by the University of Picardy, one otherwise well-informed researcher affirmed in a peremptory way that Boehme wishes "with hate and fury, to set reason and understanding against each other."[12] But this is absurd. His opposition is not to reason itself, but to *dead* reason, that which is detached from all experience and born of purely mechanical mental association. Quite the contrary, Boehme is a lover of reason and

---

* AUTHOR'S NOTE: The word "qualifieth" means, according to Louis Claude de Saint-Martin in his French translation of The Aurora (L'Aurore naissante), "the active and simultaneous gathering of different faculties, which results in a mutual impregnation."

intelligence, and this book is precisely a testimony to that. But the rationality found in his writing is a living rationality, rooted in experience. What did those twelve years of silence represent if not sacrifice in the name of reason? Why else did he write so many books, if not to try to explain, analyze, and rationalize that experience? Certainly this kind of reason is far superior to that which we have become accustomed to from the glib spokesmen of this century who are prophets of nothingness and emptiness, priests of nihilism, positivism, and mechanistic determinism.

The rationality of Boehme's work can be perceived through the metaphor of the tree, which recurs often in his writings: "The garden of this tree signifieth the *world*; the soil or mould signifieth *nature*; the stock of the tree signifies the *stars*; by the *branches* are meant the *elements*; the fruit which grow on this tree signify *men*; the sap in the tree denoteth the pure *Deity*."[13] In taking up this metaphor of the tree, Antoine Faivre grasps the contemporary importance of the rationality of Boehme's work: "One can describe in a thousand ways a single tree, but perhaps the descriptions all swing between two poles: a tree completely naked and abstract, or a tree laden with a living luxuriance. To the tree of Descartes, I would oppose this one of Boehme. . . . Which means first of all to see to it that our Western tree remains indeed alive, loaded with richly colored foliage and fruit; that the sap nourishes it and permeates it; that it no longer resembles a dead tree in a wintry countryside, like a formalized, abstract image of bloodless being."[14] This is an important contemporary gamble, for what is at stake is our own life and the life of our planet. What Boehme has written about his epoch remains completely valid for our own world: "The *holy light* is nowadays accounted a mere history and bare knowledge, and that the spirit *will not work* therein; and yet they *suppose* that is faith which they profess with their *mouths*."[15]

Jacob Boehme often declared himself a "simple man,"[16] and he was baffled and astonished by the totality of his work, which imposed itself on him as an urgent necessity. In fact, nothing seemed to predispose him to this fundamental "opening" of 1600. What exactly was the nature of this opening? From where did this extraordinary flow of data come, since it was certainly not drawn from reading the few books present in his home? What is the mechanism by which reason succeeds in deciphering the results of an experience which is on the whole irrational, without betraying it? In the current state of understanding, it would be vain to try to respond to these questions. One might well invoke the term "imaginal," introduced by Henry Corbin,[17] to designate the truly imaginary—the creative, visionary, essential, fundamental; without this *vision*, the real dissolves in an endless chain of veiled, deforming, mutilating images.

The challenge Boehme gambled on was, and remains, crucial—to reconcile opposing principles while preserving their specificity: the rational and the irrational, matter and spirit, finality and endlessness, good and evil, freedom and law, determinism and indeterminacy, the imaginary and the real—concepts which appear, in the context of his philosophy, merely as laughably poor approximations of far greater ideas.

Such a philosophy of contradictions, based primarily on inner experience, could express itself only in an appropriate language, distinct from ordinary, discursive language founded on sound Aristotelian logic. So it is not surprising that even lovers of Boehme's work are baffled by the language he used. Alexandre Koyré, for example, considered Boehme "a barbarian."[18] He sees his language as "embarrassing and stammering": "Boehme, as we have said, is one of the most enigmatic thinkers in the universe, and his books are perhaps the most badly written in existence. . . . To express himself, Boehme writes as he speaks, and speaks only in the way he thinks. The spoken word is for him definitely not an apparatus of conceptual notation; it is the living expression of a living reality."[19] Koyré adds that "Boehme speaks of everything in relation to everything else. Each of his works is a complete exposition of his whole system; and the repetitions are as frequent as the contradictions. . . . No one—except perhaps Paracelsus—speaks a language so barbaric, so clumsy."[20]

Boehme himself recognized the difficulties of a language adapted to his philosophy: "O that I had but the pen of man, and were able therewith to write down the spirit of knowledge. I can but stammer of the great mysteries like a child that is beginning to speak; so very little can the earthly tongue express what the spirit comprehendeth and understandeth; yet I will venture to try whether I may procure some to go about to seek the Pearl, whereby also I might labour in the works of

God, in my paradisical garden of roses; for the longing of the eternal matrix driveth me on to write and exercise myself in this my knowledge."[21]

The miracle is that Boehme did rediscover for himself a language suitable to his philosophy: the language of symbolism, which is, after all, commonly used in traditional thought. "The symbol is. . . . a representation which makes a hidden meaning apparent; it is the epiphany of a mystery,"[22] Gilbert Durand has written. The symbol brings about the unity of opposites, and, in order to be understood, presupposes the interaction of subject and object. It is founded on the logic of the included middle, which demands a language that breaks with everyday, "natural" language.

The symbol is a marvelous living organism which helps us read the world. It never has an ultimate or exclusive meaning. Its precision consists just in this fact, that it is capable of embracing an unlimited number of aspects of reality. We are thus obliged to accept the relativity of our way of looking at it: this relativity can be present only if the symbol is conceived of as in movement and if we ourselves experience it. Symbolism entails a decreasing entropy of language, a growing order, an augmentation of information and comprehension, as it crosses different levels of reality.

This is why it seems to me that one must read the works of Jacob Boehme for oneself to become convinced of the precision of his language. Even if it is almost unanimously admitted by specialists in Boehme's work that *The Aurora* is only a "first sketch" of his philosophic system,[23, 24] I am tempted to believe, with Hegel, that *The Aurora* remains his fundamental text, for, at least from my point of view, it is there that the symbolic approach of Boehme manifests itself in all its richness and splendor. The other books of Boehme, while stating with more precision the ideas already presented in *The Aurora* and even introducing certain new ideas, represent, in my opinion, an effort at rationalization in a language closer to binary logic, through a *partial* acceptance of symbols. This explains, perhaps, the greater fascination that they can hold for the modern Western reader. But, after all, the work of Boehme forms a whole, and the partial acceptance of symbols is almost as enriching as the shock produced by the encounter with their full manifestation.

NOTES

1. Alexandre Koyré, *La Philosophie de Jakob Boehme* (Paris: Vrin, 1971), p. 51.
2. *The Aurora*, translated into English by John Sparrow, original edition published in 1656. (London: John M. Watkins, 1960, o.p.). [TRANSLATOR'S NOTE: In the original French edition, Nicolescu uses the standard French translation of this text, *L'Aurora naissante*, translated by Le Philosophe Inconnu [Louis Claude de Saint-Martin] (Milan: Arché, 1977). The verse/paragraph numbers within each chapter vary widely between the French edition and the Sparrow English translation. References in these notes are to the Sparrow edition, with chapter numbers in Roman numerals followed by a colon, then verse numbers in Arabic numbers; page numbers of the Sparrow translation are also cited, designated by "p." or "pp." Occasional mention will be made of the French translation if variances with the Sparrow translation are of special interest. Many of these references appear in fuller context in the Appendix of selected writings by Boehme which forms the second half of this book.]
3. Jacob Boehme, letter to Caspar Lindner, in *Jacob Boehme: Essential Readings*, edited and introduced by Robin Waterfield (Wellingborough, England: Crucible/Thorsens, 1989), p. 64.
4. *Aurora*, XIX:13-14, 16; pp. 488-489.
5. *Ibid.*, XIII:24; p. 314.
6. *Ibid.*, III:112; p. 87.
7. *Ibid.*, XXV:6; p. 659.
8. Jacob Boehme, *Concerning the Three Principles of the Divine Essence*, translated by John Sparrow, 1648 (London: John M. Watkins, 1910, o.p.), XXIV:1; pp. 658-659.
9. *Aurora*, X:45; pp. 217-218.
10. *Ibid.*, XXIII:83; p. 631.
11. *Three Principles*, Appendix:23-24; pp. 769-770.
12. Heinz R. Schmitz, *L'Expérience mystique de Jakob Boehme et son project philosophique*, in *Jakob Boehme*, notes to a colloquium organized by Centre d'Études et de Recherches Interdisciplinaires de Chantilly (C.E.R.I.C.), (Paris: Vrin, 1979), p. 23.
13. *Aurora*, Preface: 7; p. 3.
14. Antoine Faivre, *La Critique boehmienne de Franz von Baader (Contribution à l'étude de l'influence de Jakob Boehme en Allemagne)*, in *Jakob Boehme*, C.E.R.I.C colloquium notes, pp. 148-149.
15. *Aurora*, XX:13; p. 524.
16. *Ibid.* [TRANSLATOR'S NOTE: The French translation, *"par un homme simple"* (*L'Aurore naissante*, II:46; p. 65) can indeed be rendered "by a simple man," though the Sparrow translation (II:80; p. 65) opts for "in simplicity."]
17. Henry Corbin, *Mundus imaginalis ou l'imaginaire et l'imaginal*, Conference of the Colloquium on Symbolism, Paris, 1964; text reedited in Henry Corbin, *Face de Dieu, face de l'homme*, «herméneutique et soufisme» (Paris: Flammarion, 1983).
18. Koyré, p. 503.
19. *Ibid.*, p. xv.
20. *Ibid.*, p. xi.
21. *Three Principles*, VII:16; p. 96.
22. Gilbert Durand, *L'Imagination symbolique* (Paris: Quadrige/P.U.F., 1984), p. 13.
23. Koyré, pp. xi-xii.
24. Even Louis Claude de Saint-Martin, the faithful translator of Boehme, considered *The Aurora* "the most informed of his works" in his Translator's Note to the French edition, *L'Aurore naissante* (Milan: Arché, 1977), p. 8.

CHAPTER TWO

Structure and Self-Organization in the Boehmian Universe

OR A contemporary reader, I think that perhaps the main interest in the writings of Jacob Boehme springs from a single idea which serves as the axis of his cosmology: namely, that everything which exists is ruled by a very small number of general laws. Boehme presents this in a strict, formal schematic diagram, which he proposes as an interpretation of our world, of the entire cosmos, and even of God himself. The conceptual plan is based on the *interaction* between a threefold logic or structure and a sevenfold, self-organizing cycle or process. The implications of such a plan are considerable in discussing such modern problems as freedom versus constraint, determinism versus indeterminacy, order versus chaos, and evolution versus involution, and we shall analyze these in detail.

The idea of a very small number of general laws is, from the start, extremely interesting: it establishes a new method of approaching reality which can be called "hypothetical/deductive." Foreseen by Kepler and established by Boehme, this method is found in science up to the present day: a certain limited number of laws—often very abstract, mathematical, and removed from directly observable reality—is postulated; the consequences of these laws are deduced; and *then* these consequences are compared to experienced data. The reverse method, by which the attempt is made to deduce general laws by starting with experienced data, belongs to sciences which are not yet mathematized or formalized.

Moreover, the fact that Kepler (1571-1630) and Galileo (1564-1642) are the contemporaries of Boehme (1575-1624) does not seem to be pure historical coincidence. Their works represent three different branches of the same common trunk of Christian thought. It is a question of three different crystallizations of one and the same cultural and spiritual environment: Boehme, the heretic of Christian thought; Kepler, the man of transition between traditional thought and modern scientific thought; and Galileo, the iconoclast and acknowledged founder of modern science.

One of the principal theses of this book is precisely the idea that Christian thinking on the Trinity—of which Boehme's doctrine stands at the apex, in my opinion—constitutes the compost which has allowed the birth of modern science. The question, "Why was modern science born in the West?" is thus illuminated by a rather unexpected light.

A: THE THREEFOLD STRUCTURE

In the cosmology of Boehme, reality is structured in three parts, determined by the action of three principles: "Now thus the eternal light, and the virtue of the light, or the heavenly paradise, moveth in the eternal darkness; and the darkness cannot comprehend the light; for they are two several Principles; and the darkness longeth after the light, because that the spirit beholdeth itself therein, and because the divine virtue is manifested in it. But though it hath not comprehended the divine virtue and light, yet it hath continually with great lust lifted up itself towards it, till it hath kindled the root of the fire in itself, from the beams of the light of God; and there arose the third Principle: And it hath its original out of the first Principle, out of the dark matrix, by the speculating of the virtue [or power] of God."[1]

These three principles are independent, but at the same time they all three interact *at once*: they engender each other, while each remaining distinct. The dynamic of their interaction is a *dynamic of contradiction*: one could speak of a negative force corresponding to the darkness, a positive force corresponding to the light, and a reconciling force corresponding to what Boehme called "extra-generation." It is a question of a contradiction among three poles, of three polarities radically opposed but nevertheless linked, in the sense that none of the three can exist without the other two.

The three principles have a *virtual* quality, for they exist outside our space-time continuum. As a result they are, in themselves, invisible, untouchable, immeasurable: "We understand, then, that the divine Essence in threefoldness in the unground* dwells in itself, but generates to itself a ground within itself . . . though this is not to be understood as to being, but as to a threefold spirit, where each is the cause of the birth of the other. And this threefold spirit is not measurable, divisible or fathomable; for there is no place found for it, and it is at the same time the unground of eternity, which gives birth to itself within itself in a ground."[2] The foundation of the Trinity is "subject to no locality, nor limit [number], nor place. It hath no place of its rest. . . ."[3]

It is important to stress that it is exactly this process of contradiction which allows *manifestation*. The hidden God (*Deus absconditus*) is not pure transcendence. Through the two other poles of this ternary contradiction, he can show himself, he can manifest, he can respond to the *wish to understand himself*. Thus the three forces corresponding to the three principles will be present in every phenomenon of reality: "And no place or position can be conceived or found where the spirit of the tri-unity is not present, and in every being; but hidden to the being, dwelling in itself, as an essence that at once fills all and yet dwells not in being, but itself has a being in itself. . . ."[4] God hidden thus becomes God manifest (*Deus revelatus*).

In this context, it is extremely interesting to remark the role that Boehme attributes to our own world.

The three principles engender three different worlds which moreover are overlapping—the world of fire, the world of light, and the exterior world: "And we are thus to understand a threefold Being, or three worlds in one another. The first is the fire-world, which takes its rise from the *centrum naturae*. . . . And the second is the light-world which dwells in freedom in the unground, out of Nature, but proceeds from the fire-world. . . . It dwells in fire, and the fire apprehends it not. And this is the middle world. . . . The third world is the outer, in which we dwell by the outer body with the external works and

---

* TRANSLATOR'S NOTE: *Boehme's term "unground"—*Ungrund *in German and* sans-fond *in French—refers to this mysterious "bottomless state" which at the same time serves as the base or foundation or ground where the Trinity dwells.*

beings. It was created from the dark world and also from the light-world. . . ."[5]

The exterior world, our world, appears as if it were a world of true *reconciliation*. It is not the world of the Fall, the world of man's guilt, of his downfall into matter. As Pierre Deghaye remarks pertinently, our world is a world of reparation: "The body of Lucifer is set on fire and it is destroyed. But this body was the universe before ours. It is the result of this catastrophe and in order to repair it that our world was created. Our world is the *third principle*."[6]

All the grandeur of our world resides in the incarnation of these three principles.

First of all, the threefold structure of reality is inscribed in man himself. Man *is* the actualization of this threefold structure: " . . . so also in like manner is every *mass* or *seed* of the *Ternary* or Trinity *in every* man,"[7] Boehme tells us. Human nature, merging the three principles, "understands therefore, at least potentially, the totality of divine manifestation."[8] What man makes of this human nature is, of course, a whole other story. In our modern world, man has forgotten that he is potentially the incarnation of three principles. The very words "three principles," not to mention their meaning, seem to us strange and absurd. We are, evidently, far from the work of spiritual alchemy, based on the balance of our own threefoldness, a work to which Boehme invites us, and which alone could give this world a real meaning. Otherwise our world is dead, absurd, accidental.

But what interests us here in the first place is the manifestation of the threefold structure of all the phenomena of Nature. Of course, one must not confuse "nature"[9] and "threefoldness": "*Nature* and the *Ternary* are not one and the same; they are distinct, though the Ternary dwelleth in nature, but unapprehended, and yet is an eternal band. . . ."[10] But in every phenomenon of Nature threefoldness per-petually appears. The Trinity, this "triumphing, springing, moveable being" is the "*eternal mother of nature*."[11] Even if the three principles are enclosed "in no time nor place,"[12] they manifest themselves none-theless in space and time. The third principle has a crucial role in this manifestation; it is what "contains the fiat, the creative word of God."[13] Everything becomes a trace, a sign of threefoldness: man, the planets, the stars, the elements. The alliance between nature and threefoldness is eternal, but man has the choice between discovering and living this alliance or forgetting, ignoring, and therefore disrupting it.

One thus understands the deep relationship between the thought of Boehme and that of Galileo, even if it is implicit and surprising, for their languages are very different. When Galileo points out the importance of experimental observation, separating experiment from sentient evidence (that furnished by the sense organs), he is very close to Boehme, for whom nature is a manifestation of divinity, and insofar as it is a manifestation, is measurable and observable. Both of them, like Kepler as well, are haunted by the idea of *laws* and *invariance*. The idea that it must be possible to reproduce phenomena, fundamental for the methodology of modern science, comes in here. The "new science" does not concern itself with singular phenomena but with those which are repeatable and which submit to a mathematic formalization. Galileo, like Boehme, did not identify human reason with divine reason. Maurice Clavelin points out that the position of Galileo "is lucid: created by an infinite being, the world is on the scale of his reason, not human reason, which understands it only within the limitations of its capacities, that is, through what it has in common with divine reason; mathematics is precisely in this position."[14]

But the difference between the two approaches, that of Galileo and that of Boehme, is also of paramount importance. For Galileo, every divine "cause" must be excluded in the formulation of a scientific theory, while for Boehme the comprehension of reality must take into account the *participation* of the divine in the processes of our world. The mathematics of Galileo is strictly quantitative, while that of Boehme is qualitative, of a symbolic order.

Since Nature has a double nature, so also does modern science. Modern science has been developing itself for several centuries on the path traced by Galileo instead of the far more obscure and complex one implicit in the works of Boehme. Galileo's success was staggering, as much on the level of experiment as on that of theory. His technological applications, demonstrating the mastery of man over nature, seemed to show the indisputable accuracy of this approach. Founded on binary logic, that of "Yes" *or* "No," modern science reached its peak in the nineteenth century, in a scientistic ideology

proclaiming that science alone, human reason alone, had the exclusive right-of-way to truth and reality (though the position of Galileo
was, as we have seen, quite different: non-positivist and non-
scientistic). The scientistic ideology began to fall apart at the birth of
quantum physics, with the discovery of a level of reality that clearly
differs from our own; this, in order to be understood, seemed to
demand a threefold logic, that of the included middle. [15] Moreover, an
unexpected encounter seems to be coming about just now between
modern physics and traditional symbolic thought. I have analyzed
these aspects at length in my book, *Nous, la particule et le monde* [16] and
I ask the reader to refer to that in order to avoid too many annoying
repetitions here. In any case, the resurgence of *meaning** in modern
physics, [17] is the sign of the double nature of modern science: by
excluding meaning from its domain, modern science rediscovered it,
by means of its own internal dynamic, on its own road.

Will there then be a return to the ideas of Boehme? It would be
hazardous to formulate any such affirmation. But what seems certain
to me is the current necessity for formulating a new Philosophy of
Nature. Understanding Boehme's work thus has a real immediacy in
this context today. A comparison between his idea of threefoldness
and that of modern thinkers such as Stéphane Lupasco or Charles
Sanders Peirce [18] would thus be highly instructive but it goes beyond
the framework of this book. It is sufficient to say here that astonish-

---

* AUTHOR'S NOTE: *The French word "le sens" ("meaning") has to be understood here in a very general philosophical, metaphysical, and experiential way. At its
most basic, "meaning" refers to the fact that many processes which initially seem
chaotic or disordered may, if properly studied, be seen to have a significance or
direction that reveals the presence of order. In this sense, "meaning" and "laws" are
intimately correlated. In a deeper way, and especially in Boehme's writings, "meaning" refers to the unitive interaction between different levels of reality, in a harmonious, evolutionary movement. More precisely, "meaning" is the contradictory
encounter between presence and absence, things sacred and profane. In our physical
universe, since consciousness is thought to be present only on the planet Earth, the
individual and mankind have a cosmic role: to simultaneously discover and produce
"meaning." Through his body, senses, and sensations, man becomes the cosmic
instrument of "meaning." Experiences and experiments are two facets of discovering
"meaning." This is why the study of the universe and the study of man are
complementary.*

ing correspondences can be established between the threefoldness of Boehme, the triad of Lupasco (actualization, potentialization, and the T-state, the "included middle"), and the triad of Peirce ("firstness, secondness, and thirdness," as he calls them). Boehme speaks of "three worlds," Lupasco of "three matters," and Peirce of "three universes." Indeed, the different triads evoked are far from identical. The source of threefold thinking in Boehme, Lupasco, and Peirce is equally different: an inner experience on Boehme's part, quantum physics for Lupasco, and mathematical graph theory for Peirce. But one and the same law seems to manifest itself, under different facets, in all who think in threes, and it is that which produces the threefold structure of reality, in all its manifestations. We are left to understand how a virtual structure can set in motion the different processes of reality.

B: THE SEVENFOLD SELF-ORGANIZATION OF REALITY

If threefoldness concerns the inner dynamics of all systems, seven-foldness is, according to Boehme, the basis, in its inexhaustible rich-ness, for the *manifestation* of all processes. Sevenfoldness functions in continual *interaction* with threefoldness: it is precisely this interaction which furnishes the key to a full comprehension of reality, at least in the view which Boehme proposes to us.

But, first of all, why choose the number seven? In the beginning it is difficult to understand why any number, even on the level of symbolic thought, should be more important than any other, in an absolute and definitive way. Why, for example, should the number 7 exclude all interest in the numbers 4 or 9 or 137 or 10^{10}? Of course, the mystic, theological, or symbolic value of the number seven is well known. Alexander Koyré's thesis[19] provides an almost exhaustive list of the different meanings of the number seven which could be applied, more or less, to Boehme's sevenfoldness: the seven lights and the seven angels of the Apocalypse, the seven lower sephiroth of the Kabbalah, the seven alchemical processes, the seven planets (a favorite hypoth-esis of Koyré), and so forth.

Personally I think one can demonstrate that all these are false trails. Correspondences between the different meanings of sevenfoldness could certainly be found, but I believe, for reasons I will explain later, that Boehme had no exterior source of inspiration for his concept of sevenfoldness other than his own vision. Moreover, sevenfoldness asserts itself in the philosophy of Boehme as a relentlessly logical consequence (following symbolic logic, of course) of one of the keystones of his thinking: that the basis of all manifestation must be in perpetual interaction with threefoldness.

It is amusing to ascertain that it is precisely this interaction which has plunged many of Boehme's commentators, as Koyré told us, "into the most cruel difficulty."[20] Koyré himself speaks of the "unhappy diagram of seven spirits that Boehme maintains against all odds."[21] He also says: "it would not be easy to classify these seven powers into three principles and to coordinate them to the three persons of the Trinity, but Boehme was never able to abandon this sevenfold framework."[22] Very fortunately, I would be tempted to add.

I do not pretend to offer a unique and definitive solution to this enigma, but I believe I can give a perfectly coherent reading of it, on the level of symbolic logic, from Boehme's own texts alone.

For Boehme, "*God is the God of order* . . . Now as there are in him *chiefly* seven qualities, whereby the *whole* divine being is driven on, and sheweth itself infinitely in these seven qualities, and yet these seven qualities are the chief or *prime* in the infiniteness, whereby the divine birth or geniture stands eternally in its order unchangeably."[23] Every process of reality thus will be ruled by seven qualities,* seven spirit-sources, seven stages, seven patterns.

The names which Boehme attributes to these seven qualities are poetic and highly evocative, but they can appear somewhat naive and

---

AUTHOR'S NOTE: Since "quality" is a key word in the cosmology of Boehme, it cannot be understood through any dictionary-type definition. Boehme's seven qualities are the intermediate, active, informational energies which give shape to all the various levels of reality. It is important to stress that the seven qualities are each generated by a particular interaction of the Three Principles. This explains a paradoxical and crucial property of these seven qualities: they are always the same, even though they adapt to the given level of materiality on which they are acting. Different levels of materiality do not imply different levels of the seven qualities. It is precisely this property of their always remaining the same which allows the possibility of cosmic unity, through the interaction of all levels of reality. Evolution itself—cosmic evolution, evolution of the individual, or evolution of mankind—therefore becomes possible.

strange to the modern reader: Sourness, Sweetness, Bitterness, Heat, Love, Tone or Sound, and Body. But what interests us here are not the names, but *the meanings* which Boehme attributes to them in the context of sevenfoldness.

Restricted by everyday language, Boehme first adopts a linear, chronological description of how these seven qualities are linked in the sevenfold cycle, but understanding them comes through a *simultaneous* consideration of their actions. The spirit-sources all give birth to each other, yet each remains distinct. Again, only a logic of contradictions gives us access to the meaning of Boehme's sevenfoldness.

But to begin with, let us proceed, like Boehme, by stages. The three first qualities proceed from the first principle. The God of the first principle is, for us, a God who is impenetrable and unknowable. He appears to us like a God of darkness, a God of terrifying night, because he is unfathomable. One cannot even truly call him God.

An intense and bitter struggle takes place among the first three qualities to permit this God of darkness to know himself in his potentiality. Why does this struggle begin among *three* qualities and not four or six? According to Boehme, the God of darkness, once started on the road to self-knowledge, must submit to his own threefold nature.

The first quality will thus correspond to a negative force, to resistance, to a *cold fire*, responding to the desire of the God of darkness to remain what he is, independent of all manifestation. The second quality will correspond to a positive, fluid force, inclined towards manifestation and thus radically opposed to the first quality: it is like what Boehme called a "furious goad." And then the third quality appears like a reconciling force without which no opening towards manifestation would be possible. The God of the first principle therefore will engage himself in a gigantic struggle with himself. Nicolas Berdiaeff speaks rightly of a "divine tragedy" in the mystery of creation.[24] It is quite simply a question of the *death of God* to himself inasmuch as he is the God of pure transcendence: "Boehme's God dies before he is born," writes Pierre Deghaye.[25] This is an idea which by itself was enough to horrify the dogmatic theologians of the day and allow them to classify Boehme easily as a heretic.

The merciless struggle among the first three qualities produces a true "wheel of anguish." The world of the first triad of sevenfoldness is a "dark valley,"[26] a virtual hell. Boehme speaks of "an anxious *horrible* quaking, a trembling, and a sharp, opposite, contentious generating."[27] Something must happen to allow the "childbirth," the passage to life, to manifestation.

It is precisely at this point, when the wheel of anguish turns frantically on itself, in a chaotic, infernal whirlwind, that a *principle of discontinuity* must be manifested, to open the way for true evolutionary movement. This principle of discontinuity is none other than *the third principle*, which appears as the *fiat of manifestation*, the creative word of God. Boehme calls this discontinuity a "flash": "Behold, without the flash all the seven spirits were a dark valley. . . ."[28] The insane movement of the wheel of anguish stops in order to transform itself into harmonious movement. It is now that life can be born, that God is born. The fiat of manifestation, generated by the third principle, becomes an integral part (although merely *virtual*, because it corresponds to an invisible interruption on the level of manifestation) of the second triad of the sevenfold cycle, which equally includes the fourth and fifth qualities: "Now these four spirits move themselves in the flash, for all the four become living therein, and so now the power of these four riseth up in the flash, as if the *life* did rise up, and the *power* which is risen up in the flash is the love, which is the *fifth spirit*. That power moveth so very pleasantly and amiably in the flash, as if a dead spirit did become living, and was suddenly in a moment set into great clarity or *brightness*."[29] The fact that the fourth and the fifth qualities are intimately linked to the lightning flash, and therefore to the third principle, is thus clearly affirmed.

The *cold fire* of the first triad thus transforms itself into a hot fire from which light can burst forth: "The fourth property thus plays the role of a turntable or pivot of transmutation for the whole system," Jean-François Marquet has written.[30] I would be tempted to say rather that the turntable is located in the *interval* between the third and the fourth quality, for it is there that the action of the fiat of life, of manifestation, takes place.

But "birth" does not mean a complete manifestation of the light. With the second triad, God is born, he becomes conscious of himself, but he does not yet manifest himself fully. A *second principle of discontinuity* must intervene so that the evolutionary movement can con-

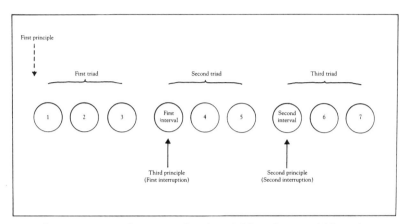

First principle

First triad

Second triad

Third triad

1   2   3   First interval   4   5   Second interval   6   7

Third principle
(First interruption)

Second principle
(Second interruption)

The interaction between the threefold and sevenfold cycles.

tinue. The fiat of affirmation, of the light fully revealed, the *heavenly fiat* is necessarily the action of the second principle. "The second *fiat* is found at the fifth degree," Pierre Deghaye correctly affirms.[31] More precisely, it is found in *the interval* between the fifth and the sixth quality.

The intervention of the second principle generates a new triad of manifestation ("triad," for each principle must submit itself to its own threefold structure). This next triad is composed of three elements: one virtual element (the interruption generated by the second principle) and two qualities: Tone or Sound, and Body.

The sixth quality is that of heavenly joy, like a joyful sound which runs through the whole manifestation: "Now the *sixth* generating in God is *when* the *spirits*, in their birth or geniture, thus *taste* one of another. . . . whereby and wherein the *rising joy* generateth itself, from whence the *tone* or *tune* existeth. For from the touching and moving the living spirit generateth itself, and that same spirit presseth through all births or generatings, very *inconceivably* and incomprehensibly to the birth or geniture, and is a very richly joyful, pleasant, lovely sharpness, like melodious, sweet music. And now when the birth generateth, then it *conceiveth* or apprehendeth the light, and speaketh or inspireth the light again into the birth or geniture through the moving spirit."[32] It is at the level of the sixth quality that Boehme placed language, discernment, and beauty.[33]

As for the seventh quality, it corresponds to full manifestation, to the "body" of God, which is none other than nature itself: "Now the seventh form, or the seventh spirit in the divine power, is *nature*, or the issue or *exit* from the other six. . . . [This seventh spirit] is the *body* of all the spirits, wherein they generate themselves as in a body: Also out of this spirit all *figures*, shapes and forms are imaged or fashioned."[34] The seventh spirit "encompasseth the other six, and generateth them again: for the *corporeal* and *natural* being consisteth in the seventh."[35] The loop is thus closed: the seventh quality rejoins the first, but on another level, that of manifestation. The line changes into a circle: paradoxically, in the philosophy of Jacob Boehme, the Son gives birth to the Father.

I confess I do not understand the perplexity of Boehme's interpreters regarding the interaction between threefoldness and sevenfoldness, but the interpretation that I propose seems to me coherent, rational, and completely conforming to Boehme's texts.

The cycle of manifestation ought to demonstrate the full power of threefoldness. This full power obtains when each of the three principles manifests its own threefold structure, a structure which results from the perpetual interaction between each principle and the other two principles. If each principle does not have a threefold structure, the interaction between the three principles will be mutilated or annihilated. As a result, the cycle of manifestation must include *nine* elements ($3 \times 3 = 9$). But two of the elements are virtual, invisible — they correspond to two interruptions. Therefore on the visible, natural level, the manifestation cycle would have to be a *sevenfold* structure ($9 - 2 = 7$).

But, taken in its entirety (including therefore the two intervals where the interruptions take place that are produced by the action of the second and third principles), this cycle has a *ninefold* structure. One sees therefore the fundamental importance that Boehme accorded to the number nine, associating it with what he called the *Tincture*: "Boehme saw the temporal Universe as permeated by an immense current of life (*Tincture*), which, born of the *Principium* or *Centrum* (*Separator*) of Divinity, discharges itself upon the world, penetrates it, incarnates itself in it, and vivifying it, brings it back to

God . . . The *Tincture*, which is the number nine, is the pure element, the divine element."[36]

Two supplementary remarks need to be mentioned for the clarification of certain aspects of the cycle of manifestation.

First, we have spoken of two interruptions, of two *fiats*, linked to the
second and third principles. Why not speak of a third interruption,
linked to the first principle? Certainly "in every will the flash standeth
again to [make an] opening," as Boehme has written.[37] But, the God
of the first principle is completely ungraspable by himself. To speak of
a *fiat* bound to his will would be pure verbiage. On the other hand, this
God makes himself concrete in the first triad of the sevenfold cycle.

Secondly, the inversion between the action of the third principle
and that of the second principle in the course of the sevenfold cycle
seems very significant to me: again, the third principle, that which
rules our own world, acts as a reconciling force between the first and
the second.

It also might be instructive to make a comparative study between
the cosmology of Boehme and that of G. I. Gurdjieff (1877-1949). As
with Boehme, the fundamental laws of the universe are, in the cosmology of Gurdjieff, a Law of Three and a Law of Seven, and their
interaction is expressed as a Law of Nine.[38, 39] The threefoldness,
sevenfoldness, and ninefoldness of Gurdjieff are not, indeed, the same
as those of Boehme; but their comparative study could reveal interesting sidelights. We cannot attempt such a study here. But it is surprising to remark that not one of the numerous analysts of Gurdjieff's
ideas speaks of the striking analogy between his laws and those of
Boehme. Even his most informed biographer, James Webb,[40] cites
Boehme only casually.

Boehme's sevenfold structure penetrates all levels of reality. The
birth of God is repeated endlessly throughout all these levels, in
"signatures" or "traces." He writes: "The seven spirits of God, in the
circumference and *space*, contain or comprehend heaven and this
world; also the *wide breadth and depth* without and beyond the heavens,
even above and beneath the world, and in the world. . . . They
contain also *all* the *creatures* both in heaven and in this world. . . .
Out of and from the same *body* of the seven spirits of God are *all things*
made and produced, all angels, all devils, the heaven, the earth, the

stars, the elements, men, beasts, fowls, fishes; all worms, wood, trees, also stones, herbs and grass, and *all* whatsoever is."[41]

At a certain level of reality, the sevenfold cycle can develop fully, can stop, or can even involve; the different systems belong to a level of reality that enjoys the freedom of *self-organization*. The divine *Nature* and its evolution is predetermined insofar as *potentiality* is concerned. But the interruption characterizing the sevenfold cycle introduces an element of indeterminacy, of liberty, of choice. As Koyré remarks: "The lightning flash is that of freedom introducing itself into Nature, which is the opposite of freedom."[42] In Boehme's universe, determinism and indeterminacy, constraint and freedom coexist contradictorily.

Is not the God of darkness, the magical source of all reality, in himself, the Great Indeterminacy? But his "hunger and desire is after substance,"[43] and he is obliged to accept a certain determinism, a certain "contraction." As Deghaye points out, "In the Kabbalah of Isaac Luria, there is a similar phenomenon: at the origin of all worlds, the Infinite contracts itself and thus begins the true drama, in the bosom of Divinity."[44] It is on this "divine tragedy" that the greatness of our own world is founded: that of the full evolution of man. The self-knowledge of God thus rejoins the self-knowledge of man.

NOTES

1. Jacob Boehme, *Concerning the Three Principles of the Divine Essence*, translated by John Sparrow, 1648 (London: John M. Watkins, 1910, o.p.), VII:25; p. 100.
2. Jacob Boehme, *Sex Puncta Theosophica or High and Deep Grounding of Six Theosophic Points: An Open Gate to All the Secrets of Life Wherein the Causes of All Being Become Known*, written in the year 1620. Translated into English by John Rolleston Earle as part of *Six Theosophic Points and Other Writings* (New York: Alfred A. Knopf, 1920, o.p.), I:20,21; p. 18.
3. *Three Principles*, XIV:84; pp. 298-299.
4. *Six Theosophic Points*, I:21; pp. 18-19.
5. *Ibid.*, II:32-34, 37; pp. 39-40.
6. Pierre Deghaye, *La Naissance de Dieu ou La doctrine de Jakob Boehme* (Paris: Albin Michel, Collection *Spiritualités Vivantes*, 1985), p. 156.
7. *The Aurora*, translated into English by John Sparrow, original edition published in 1656. (London: John M. Watkins, 1960, o.p.), XXVI:106; p. 711.
8. Deghaye, p. 57.
9. See "The Double Nature of Nature" in Chapter Three.
10. *Aurora*, XI:104; p. 257.

11. *Ibid.*, II:59, 60; p. 61.
12. *Six Theosophic Points*, II:2; p. 131.
13. Gerhard Wehr, *Jakob Boehme*, translated into French from German by Paul Kellser, in *Jakob Boehme* (Paris: Albin Michel, Collection *Cahiers de l'Hermétisme*, 1977) p. 67.
14. Maurice Clavelin, *Galilée*, in *Dictionnaire des philosophes*, edited by Denis Huisman (Paris: P.U.F., 1984), pp. 999-1000.
15. Stéphane Lupasco, *L'Expérience microphysique et la pensée humaine* (Paris: P.U.F., 1941); *Le Principe d'antagonisme et la logique de l'énergie* (Paris: Le Rocher, Collection *L'Esprit et la Matière*, 1987), preface by Basarab Nicolescu; *Les Trois Matières* (Paris: Cohérence, 1982).
16. Basarab Nicolescu, *Nous, la particule et le monde* (Paris: Le Mail, 1985); see, in particular, the chapter "Contemporary Physics and Western Tradition."
17. Bernard d'Espagnat, *Une Incertaine Réalité* (Paris: Gauthier-Villars, 1985).
18. Charles S. Peirce, *Selected Writings (Values in a Universe of Chance)*, edited by Philip P. Wiener (New York: Dover, 1966).
19. Alexandre Koyré, *La Philosophie de Jakob Boehme* (Paris: Vrin, 1971), pp. 125-129.
20. *Ibid.*, p. 380.
21. *Ibid.*, p. 146.
22. *Ibid.*, p. 148.
23. *Aurora*, XII:29,30; pp. 273-274.
24. Nicolas Berdiaeff, "Études sur Jakob Boehme," in his introduction to his French translation of *Mysterium Magnum* (Paris: Éditions d'Aujourd'hui, 1978), vol. I, p. 12.
25. Pierre Deghaye, "Psychologia Sacra," in *Jakob Boehme*, Albin Michel, *op. cit.*, p. 204.
26. *Aurora*, XI:14; p. 238.
27. *Ibid.*, XXIII:22; p. 617.
28. *Ibid.*, XI:14; p. 238.
29. *Ibid.*, XI:15, 16; p. 238.
30. Jean-François Marquet, "Désir et imagination," in *Jakob Boehme*, notes to a colloquium organized by Centre d'Études et de Recherches Interdisciplinaires de Chantilly (C.E.R.I.C.), (Paris: Vrin:, 1979), p. 84.
31. Deghaye, *La Naissance de Dieu*, p. 181.
32. *Aurora*, XXIII:40-43; pp. 621-622.
33. *Ibid.*, X:1; p. 207.
34. *Ibid.*, XVI:6,7; p. 410.
35. *Ibid.*, XI:85; pp. 252-253.
36. Koyré, p. 447.
37. *Three Principles*, XIV:67; p. 290.
38. P.D. Ouspensky, *In Search of the Miraculous* (New York: Harcourt Brace Jovanovich, 1949). [See especially Chapters 4-7.]
39. G.I. Gurdjieff, *All and Everything: Beelzebub's Tales to His Grandson* (New York: E.P. Dutton, 1950). [See especially Chapters 17 and 40.]
40. James Webb, *The Harmonious Circle* (New York: G.P. Putnam's Sons, 1980).
41. *Aurora*, IX:74-77; p. 203.
42. Koyré, p. 252.
43. *Six Theosophic Points*, I:27; p. 20.
44. Deghaye, *La Naissance de Dieu*, p. 33.

Das übersinn-
liche Leben
und
Göttliche Be-
schaulichkeit.

CHAPTER THREE

Must a Cosmology of Self-Creation Necessarily Be Tragic?

CCORDING to Jacob Boehme, all creation begins in suffering, on the wheel of anguish. Even God, in order to understand himself, must first die to himself so that he can be born. Certainly this "death of God" has nothing in common with that phrase invented by modern philosophers: God dies to himself in order then to *take part in* life, to show himself, to reveal all the powers which are hidden inside himself. All cosmoses, all worlds (our own included), all creatures must pass through the stages of the sevenfold cycle which begins in suffering: it is the price paid for the appearance of "light," of evolution. But does this mean the cosmology of Boehme is therefore intrinsically tragic?

This question is more timely than it first appears. Modern scientific cosmology (which concerns only our own material world), founded on the theory of the Big Bang, offers us a fascinating and baffling image of the evolution of our universe. Moreover, very often the language used (especially in so-called popularizations) seems to come out of a text by Boehme. The universe was probably, at the very beginning of the Big Bang, a ball of fire where an infernal temperature raged. An undifferentiated energy animated a shapeless mass of quarks, leptons, and other particles, described by a single interaction. This ball of fire potentially contained the whole universe. By a continual cooling, the different physical interactions happened gradually, finally giving birth to galaxies, to stars, to different suns, to planets, to life, to ourselves. It is astonishing that this growing complexity of the universe passed through extremely narrow "windows": strong restraints seem to have been brought to bear on certain physical and astrophysical quantities (the age of the universe, the values of different coupling constants that characterize the physical interactions, etc.) so that our universe might actually appear. I am referring, of course, to the celebrated "anthropic principle,"[1] which is, in my opinion,[2] a sign of a comprehensive self-consistency which seems to govern the evolution of our universe. Moreover, the idea of a spontaneous appearance of the universe runs through many important works achieved within the framework of quantum cosmology. The universe seems capable of creating itself and organizing itself, with no external intervention.

But the fundamental questions of the understanding of this evolution of the universe remain unsolved. How can we comprehend the fact that *our* time has risen out of timelessness, that our space-time continuum has been generated by something of a different nature? What purpose is served by all the very fine and precise adjustments between different physical parameters so that the universe can be such as it is? All that, in order to lead up to the death of the physical universe, either by progressive cooling (in the eventuality of an open universe, continually expanding) or by a progressive heating (in the opposite scenario of a closed universe, which will end by contracting itself incessantly)? Evidently some of these questions will be considered non-scientific, belonging instead to the domain of philosophy. But these questions are ineluctably there.

A great physicist like Steven Weinberg (who is among the rare contemporary physicists who consecrate a part of their studies to sound philosophical thought) does not hesitate to pose the problem of the *absurdity* of the universe: "It is almost irresistible for humans to believe that we have some special relation to the universe, that human life is not just a more-or-less farcical outcome of a chain of accidents reaching back to the first three minutes, but that we were somehow built in from the beginning . . . It is even harder to realize that this present universe has evolved from an unspeakably unfamiliar early condition, and faces a future extinction of endless cold or intolerable heat. The more the universe seems comprehensible, the more it also seems pointless."[3] For his part, Edgar Morin, founder of an epistemology of complexity, poses the question of the tragic character of the universe: "Isn't the growing complexity only a detour in the generalized disaster of a universe that is intrinsically and definitively tragic?"[4]

Is the universe absurd? Tragic? Maybe, if one ignores the role of life, of man and his consciousness. It is certain that modern science by itself could never respond to such questions: its own methodology limits the field of questions to those that can be answered. A new Philosophy of Nature, attuned to the considerable attainments of modern science, is cruelly lacking.

A contemporary reading of the writings of Jacob Boehme could help us on the long road in search of this new Philosophy of Nature.

A: ON THE NECESSITY OF A MIRROR: THE DOUBLE NATURE OF NATURE

There is a double meaning to the word "nature" in the works of Jacob Boehme, and to ignore that would engender an endless series of annoying confusions. What Boehme calls the "Unground" or the "Great Indeterminacy" is "outside of all nature."[5] When this Great Indeterminacy consents to respond to its own wish for self-knowledge, it simply dies and is reborn according to a *divine nature*, regulated by the sevenfold cycle. God gains consciousness of his own divinity by engaging himself in the sevenfold cycle, with its different stages: "The Father is called a holy God only in the Son . . . In the fire he is called an angry God; but in the light or love-fire he is called the holy God: and in the dark nature he is not called God."[6] Thus the body of God engenders itself, as the materialization of the sevenfold cycle. There is thus a certain degree of materiality in the body of God, subject to its own time. This "divine substance, which is the heavenly flesh in the realm of Wisdom [Sophia]"[7] gives the master key to the sevenfold cycle in the process of manifestation. This sevenfold divine cycle will be the prototype of all the other sevenfold cycles acting at different levels of reality. But if it were not a question, from the beginning, of a certain materiality, no communication would be possible among all the levels of reality. It is precisely this materiality which conditions the passage of information among all these levels. The divine nature would be locked into itself: "In the spiritual world there are only the properties of possibility," Boehme tells us.[8] The revelation, in this case, would be only a false, gratuitous, and useless revelation. It is here that the necessity for the mirror appears; that is, the appearance of other levels of reality, possessing their own degrees of materiality, which are going to make accessible the exploration of divine nature. The other worlds, among them ours, will reflect the divine life as in a mirror. But to say "mirror" is also to imply warping or "distortion." The image in the mirror is not what looks at its reflection. Thus, these other worlds will correspond to another nature—the creaturely nature. As Antoine Faivre has aptly remarked: "There are two natures, the one 'incorruptible,' the other not. . . . There are two self-manifestations of God, one eternal and not creaturely, the other creaturely. If we do not make this distinction maintained by Boehme, we fall into Pantheism."[9]

Thus Boehme uses two meanings for the word "nature," and we must distinguish the two whenever necessary. To be more precise, I am therefore going to write the word with a capital letter when I wish to indicate both meanings at once—Nature which takes in *both* the divine *and* the creaturely natures. "Nature" with a capital N thus refers to interaction among *all* levels of reality.

The interaction between these two natures explains the meaning that Boehme attributes to "God revealed": "The essences are his manifestation, and thereof alone we have ability to write; and not of the unmanifested God, who, without his manifestation, also were not known to himself."[10] It is thus that the grandeur of our own world becomes evident and one can then understand in what sense Boehme becomes ecstatic about the "wonders of the outward world."[11]

Everything, in this world, becomes a "sign"—a sign of possible evolution, of cosmic coherence: "But here thou must elevate thy mind in the *spirit*, and consider how the *whole nature*, with all the powers which are in nature, also the wideness, depth and height, also heaven and earth, and all whatsoever is therein, and all that is above the heavens, is together the *body* or corporeity of God; and the powers of the stars are the fountain veins in the natural body of God *in this world*. Thou must not conceive that in the body of the stars is the *triumphing* Holy Trinity, God. . . . But we must not so conceive as if God were not at all in the *corpus* or body of the stars, and in this world."[12]

Again, only the contradictory logic at the foundation of symbolic thought can give us access to the meanings that Boehme wants to transmit. The body of God *is* our nature, but only by a subtle and alchemical operation of correspondences. The effects and phenomena manifesting themselves in our world are certainly different from the effects and phenomena manifesting themselves in the divine world or in other worlds. But there is a link between them which is produced by the engagement of the different sevenfold cycles operating at different levels of reality. The body of God manifesting itself in our own world is a corresponding *image* to the body of God manifesting the divine nature. The purity of this image depends on *us*, on our capacity to explore and to live both our own nature and the nature called "exterior." Boehme does not confuse unity and diversity even when he says, "all creatures of the world are only one and the same thing," for he says to us at the same time that "When I take up a stone or clod of earth and look upon it, then I see that which is above and that which is below, yea, [I see] the whole world therein; only, that in each thing one property happeneth to be the chief and most manifest; according to which it is named."[13] Using the terminology of Stéphane Lupasco, one might affirm that, for Boehme, unity is potentialized, while diversity is actualized, but one could not exist without the other. Their contradictory interplay is at the very center of evolution, whether our own evolution or that of the "exterior" world. This contradiction springs from the confrontation between two centers, two points of concentration of cosmic energies: a *centrum naturae* or nature-center, which expresses the tendency towards concretization in the different material forms of nature, which can be seen, measured, and analyzed—and a *center of light*, which expresses the tendency towards spiritualization, towards communication with different levels of reality. It is by the contradictory balance between these two centers that man becomes the mirror of the universe: "for all is to be found in this world, yea in every thing that liveth and moveth. . . . The divine virtue [or power discovereth, or] beholdeth itself in all things, as it is written, *The word is near thee, even in your heart and lips*."[14]

B: INSTANTANEITY AND NON-SEPARABILITY
IN BOEHME'S COSMOLOGY

In the preceding chapter, the sevenfold cycle was described in a linear way, as a succession of chronological stages. But we have also seen that as it unfolds, the line changes itself into a circle, and at the center of the circle there appears "the heart of *light*, which the seven spirits continually generate as a light of life."[15]

The cyclical nature clarifies for us the properties of these seven qualities or energies which operate throughout the cosmos. These cosmic energies or "fountain-spirits"[16] are interdependent: they permeate each other[17] in a "continual struggle of begetting, as in a love game."[18] As a result, it is necessary to think of them as simultaneous: "*These seven* generatings *in all* are *none of them* the first, the second, or the third, or last, but they are all seven, every one of them, both the first, second, third, fourth, and last. Yet I must set them down one after another, according to a *creaturely* way and manner, otherwise thou couldst not understand it: For the *Deity* is as a wheel with seven wheels made one in another, wherein a man seeth *neither* beginning nor end."[19] The seven qualities or energies thus engender each other, each one remaining distinct, according to the predominance of one or another tendency in the process of manifestation.

Boehme thus arrived at a dazzling image of divinity as a wheel: an image charged with power that is poetic, symbolic, *and* rational. One could cite entire pages from *The Aurora* here, but I will content myself with one brief passage: "Suppose a WHEEL standing before thee, with seven *wheels* one so made in the other that it could go on *all* sides, forward, backward and cross ways, without need of any turning back or stopping. In its going, that always-one wheel, in its turning about, *generateth* the others, and yet none of them vanish out of sight, but that all seven be visible or in sight. The seven wheels always generating the *naves* in the midst or centre according to their turning about, so that the nave stand always free without alteration or removing, whether the wheels go forward or backward or cross ways or upward or downward. . . . And the seven wheels are *hooped* round with *fellies*, like a round *globe*. And yet that a man may see all the seven wheels turning round about severally apart, as also the whole *fitness* or compass of the frame, with all its fellies and spokes and naves. The *seven naves* in the midst or centre being as it were *one nave*, which doth fit everywhere in the turning about. . . ."[20]

This wheel, closed into a "spherical globe," is also *open*. By the action of the second and third principles in relation to the intervals of *discontinuity* mentioned above, the wheel contains within itself all the other wheels of the sevenfold cycle, operating at different levels of reality. Life and information flows to all these levels, but at the same time, divinity itself is nourished by the life and movement of these levels. It is there that the divinity's true self-knowledge resides, in this interaction among all conceivable sevenfold cycles, which correspond to different degrees of materiality. Thus in Boehme's cosmology, there is outlined a majestic cosmic chain, which closes on itself in a cycle without beginning or end. The universe appears as a grand whole, a vast cosmic matrix where everything is in perpetual movement and energetic relationship. This vision is astonishingly close to one which evolves from contemporary scientific thought, based on a study of natural systems.[21] Thinkers engaged in any way on this path would find a great source of inspiration and enlightenment in the writings of Boehme.

This interlocking of all the seven cycles inside each other determines the instantaneity and non-separability acting in Boehme's universe. The unity of this endless chaining together of different cycles escapes the action of time, which operates on various levels of reality; the unity simply *is*, outside of all time or space. It is in this sense that the wheel of divinity "always appears more and more *wonderful* and marvellous, with its rising up, and yet abideth also in its own place."[22]

Boehme's universe is also characterized by its non-separability. If one given sevenfold cycle is cut off from the others, the movement of the whole stops and degenerates, as if disabled. It would be very interesting to see in what measure the surprising idea of quantum non-separability, discovered theoretically as well as experimentally in the field of quantum physics, might be interpreted philosophically as a "sign" of generalized non-separability of the sort that characterizes Boehme's cosmology. Certainly one must not confuse the different levels of reality. Quantum non-separability is a precise notion (in the scientific meaning of the term) and is thus very limited in its application. According to Bernard d'Espagnat: "If the idea of an independent reality for man is to make any sense, then such a reality must be non-separable. And by 'non-separable,' it must be understood that if we conceive of reality as being made up of parts that can be localized in space, and these parts interact in certain well-established ways when they are close together, then they will continue to interact no matter what their distance from each other, in accordance with the action of instantaneous influences."[23] Boehme was moreover the first to warn us against the abusive correlation of what is "seen" with phenomena of another nature. In speaking of the characteristic properties of the components of the first triad of the septenary, he writes: "And these now have the comprehensibility or palpability, and are the birth of the *outermost* nature."[24] But we must avoid confusing these tangible qualities with other qualities or energies of the sevenfold cycle. For there we ourselves are fully implicated, by our sensibility, by our conscience, by our manner of interacting with the world. Still, nothing forbids questioning what is "seen" in a much more complex context, on the level of symbol, on the condition, of course, that this reading of the symbol is coherent, founded not on superficial analogies but on strictly exact correspondences. Such a reading is obligatory in a cosmology like that of Boehme, where everything is a "sign" of interaction with the rest of the cosmos. A "sign" is not a "symbol," and a symbol is not reality. But the *dynamic* of the sevenfold cycles in Boehme's cosmology is a marvelous symbolic instrument for deciphering the world.

C: UNITY IN DIVERSITY
AND DIVERSITY THROUGH UNITY

It is difficult to understand how Boehme arrived at reconciling "unity" and "diversity" unless we pay attention to his concept of "embodiment,"[25] in the sense of the "body" born through the completion of the sevenfold cycle. But the body of one cosmos is not the same as that of another, since the result of each cycle depends on laws belonging to that particular cosmos. But, according to Boehme, the different sevenfold cycles are in communication with one another: the different bodies would therefore be linked to each other, whether they are the body of God, the bodies of angels, the bodies of demons, or our own bodies. All the different bodies thus form a single body: "For in the innermost birth the upper and nether Deity is *one body*, and is an open gate."[26] The different configurations or different forms appearing in the different cosmoses certainly are impossible to confuse with each other, but the interlocking of the different sevenfold cycles allows a certain *relationship* to exist between these forms and configurations: "One world is in the other, and all are only one."[27] Our own body potentially contains within it the whole universe: "For the earthly body which thou bearest is one body with the whole kindled body of this world, and thy body qualifieth, mixeth or uniteth with the whole body of this world; and there is no difference between the stars and the deep, as also between the earth and thy body; it is all one body. This is the only difference, thy body is a *son* of the whole, and is in itself as the whole being itself is."[28]

It is true that "in that infiniteness of the flash, there is in every discovery of the whole in the particular (in every reflection) again a centre of such a birth as is in the whole,"[29] but at the same time, in the process of the sevenfold cycle, there are "many thousand centres without number or end."[30] This contradiction is explained by the freedom and indeterminacy which are found in each cosmos. In Boehme's universe, not everything is predetermined: far from it. God did not even foresee the fall of Lucifer. . . . Each cosmos is a determinate/indeterminate unity of contradictions. The choice or free will acting in each cosmos is what determines what direction the sevenfold cycle can take in that cosmos. *The unity* of which Boehme speaks concerns the completion of *all* the sevenfold cycles, while *the diversity* appears in the process of each individual cycle, with its fluctuations, hesitations, and distortions. Unity and diversity themselves form a contradictory pair; which one becomes actual or which one remains potential depends on *the time* operating at that particular level.

The unity of our physical world is again like a "sign" of this far greater general unity that Boehme described. In this context, it is interesting to note the proliferation of unified theories in contemporary particle physics, all of which tend toward a single description of all physical interactions. In these theories, our universe appears as a whole, from particle to cosmos. I have analyzed these theories at length elsewhere;[31] here I will only say that "unity," "unification" and even "unicity" are words which have appeared more and more often in physics in the past few years. It is also interesting to note that two contradictory aspects—the unity and diversity of physical interactions—can coexist in one and the same theory. Therefore it is perhaps no accident that the unification theory currently most in vogue—the "superstring theory"—has its historical origin in the "bootstrap" approach, a law of dynamics which states that the characteristics and attributes of a certain physical entity are the result of interactions with other particles existing in nature: a particle is what it is precisely because of all the other particles existing at the same instant.[32]

It is not just in physics that this idea of unification is more and more frequently expressed. Under different guises, it appears in other sciences as well. We can cite, for example, the "Gaïa hypothesis" of James Lovelock,[33] a fertile speculation on the scientific/ecological plane, which also has astonishing epistemological implications:[34] the earth is seen as a living organism, with its own intelligence about how to maintain its own life. It seems important to stress one aspect of both these hypotheses, in the context being discussed. When either the "bootstrap principle" or the "Gaïa hypothesis" is taken in its most general sense, it is ineffective for formulating a scientific theory or model. But if we consider them as *partial* meanings, they can lead to truly scientific approaches. Everything that occurs seems to show that what is explored by scientific methodology is only a partial aspect of an infinitely richer reality: a great number of scientific models can be founded on one and the same hypothesis, whether it be bootstrap, unification, Gaïa, or whatever, each of which has its own value in investigating the properties of natural systems. These hypotheses represent in turn individual facets of a general hypothesis of universal interdependence like that which is the central thesis of Boehme's cosmology. That very general hypothesis is still more ineffectual on the direct plane of scientific methodology: its efficacy is found instead in the formulation of a world vision which goes beyond the narrow framework of scientific methodology, without being completely disconnected from it. Such a vision operates on the symbolic plane, which can be extremely stimulating to the imagination of scientist or layman. Is not the true imagination the very source of discovery of many great scientific theories?[35]

An understanding of Boehme's concept of the *materiality* of each cosmos is needed in order to see the correspondences between his idea of unity and unity as it is spoken of in modern scientific theory. When he writes: "Further, the sun is made or generated from all the stars, and is a light taken from the whole nature, and shineth again into the whole nature of this world; it is *united* with the other stars, as if itself together with all the stars were but *one* star" [36] — one has the impression of reading the text of a modern physicist, familiar with the bootstrap and the anthropic principles, who is thus launching a new cosmic bootstrap hypothesis. The modernity of Boehme's thought is likewise linked to this idea which keeps coming back in different forms throughout his writing, that nature is not accidental but exists to teach us something about ourselves through our interactions with it. Edgar Morin takes pertinent note of the modern rebirth of the concept of Nature, which had been expelled as a "romantic phantasm" by the science of the preceding century: "At the same time that the universe is becoming strange, mysterious, frozen in space, yet burning and exploding among the stars, terrifying with its black holes which drink their own light, the rebirth is taking place of a Nature that is organic, complex, womblike, nourishing, and placental, at once enveloping man and inside of him."[37]

It is important to remember that in Boehme's cosmology the qualities of the sevenfold cycle are *energies*: they are the very source of movement. As a result a flow of energy endlessly floods the whole cosmos to insure this interaction. Nothing is "empty" in the cosmos: "The whole deep between the stars and the earth is inhabited, and not void and empty."[38]

The unity of the all the cosmoses corresponds to an energy which defies human understanding but which manifests itself on all levels: "The place where the SUN is, is such a place as you may choose or suppose *anywhere* above the earth; and if God should kindle the light by the heat, then the *whole* world would be such a mere SUN; for that same power wherein the *sun* standeth *is everywhere* all over. . . ."[39] Is the fabulous energy of the infinitely small that twentieth-century physics has succeeded in discovering on the quantum level also a "sign" of this energy of unity? In any case, it is a well-known scientific fact that the smaller the area of exploration, the greater the energy required to explore it. Everything indicates that an ever more immense energy seems to be "hidden" in tinier and tinier places (and it is a good thing that it is "hidden," given the murderous folly of mankind). Any "point" is linked with the entire universe; it is like the universe in miniature. For the sevenfold generative power is found everywhere, "even in the smallest circle that can be imagined."[40] Of course, once again, we must not confuse a "sign" with total reality. The energy that is found in the physical universe *is not* the energy of unity. In Boehme's cosmology, it is Love [the fifth quality] that is the "source of unity and intercommunication."[41]

But the energy that the physicists have succeeded in discovering on the scale of the infinitely small seems instead to draw its source, in Boehme's language, from the first triad of the sevenfold cycle, that of the "wheel of anguish."

D: SPACE AND TIME: REALITY AND ILLUSION

As has been said, each sevenfold cycle unfolds in its own time. But the unity of *all* sevenfold cycles takes place in timelessness. Therefore, any very specific time-frame appears to be an approximation or a sort of illusion—like a section of timelessness: "and time coucheth in eternity,"[42] as Boehme continually affirms.

Similarly, the space that characterizes each cosmos is an approximation, a section of the spacelessness that characterizes the unity of all cosmoses: "For the *true heaven* is everywhere, even in that very place where thou standest and goest."[43] In complete unity, "what is near and what is far are simply the same thing."[44] All of Boehme's cosmology speaks to us of the possibility of the evolution of the human soul to the point of abolition of time and space. The soul then "can now be above, and now beneath; it is not *hindered* by anything."[45] But it is a question of a potential, of a gradual approach that must be accomplished. This approach is described by the process of the seven-part cycle, which itself unfolds in a particular time. And it is this process which directly concerns us and our life. Without this gradual approach, it is not possible to reach fulfillment. Without suffering and passage through the wheel of anguish, the light can never burst forth.

The greatness of Boehme thus consists in his recognition of the value of time. He does not despise time, just as he does not despise the external world. Quite the contrary. If the external world appears to be a reconciling force between the world of shadows and the world of light, then time is necessarily the mediator between Indeterminacy and its mirror opposite. Our world is not the world in ruins, but a world in the process of repairing itself. As a result, our time is potentially a time *for ascent*, a time for revelation and accomplishment. On the level of the unity of all the cosmoses, time may appear to be an approximation, but on our own level, it is an inevitable reality, a necessary passage. The time of nature, the time of history, the time of our own evolution—each of these times has a "sense," in the double meaning of the word: significance and direction. Its direction is toward its own abolition, and its significance is the possibility of the progressive fulfillment of the sevenfold cycle. Time is truly found in eternity, as Boehme tells us: eternity is "fed" by time.

NOTES

1. For a good popularization of the anthropic principle, see John Barrow and Frank Tipler, *The Anthropic Cosmological Principle* (Oxford: Clarendon Press, 1986).
2. Basarab Nicolescu, *Nous, la particule et le monde* (Paris: Le Mail, 1985), pp. 54-58.
3. Steven Weinberg, *The First Three Minutes* (New York: Bantam Books, 1979), pp. 143-144.
4. Edgar Morin, "La Relation anthropo-bio-cosmique," to appear in *Encyclopédie philosophique* (Paris: P.U.F., forthcoming).
5. Jacob Boehme, *Mysterium Magnum*, translated by John Sparrow, 1654 (London: John M. Watkins, 1924, o.p.), VII:6; p. 36.
6. *Ibid.*, VII:14; p. 38.
7. Pierre Deghaye, "Psychologia Sacra," in *Jakob Boehme* (Paris: Albin Michel, Collection *Cahiers de l'Hermétisme*, 1977), p. 222.
8. *Mysterium Magnum*, X:7; p. 56.
9. Antoine Faivre, *La Critique boehmienne de Franz von Baader (Contribution à l'étude de l'influence de Jakob Boehme en Allemagne)*, in *Jakob Boehme*, notes to a colloquium by the Centre d'Études et de Recherches Interdisciplinaires de Chantilly (C.E.R.I.C.), (Paris: Vrin, 1979), p. 141.
10. *Mysterium Magnum*, V:10; p. 24.
11. *Ibid.*, VIII:7; p. 41.
12. *The Aurora*, translated into English by John Sparrow, original edition published in 1656. (London: John M. Watkins, 1960, o.p.), II:28-30; pp. 55,56.
13. *Mysterium Magnum*, II:6; p. 5.
14. Jacob Boehme, *Concerning the Three Principles of the Divine Essence*, translated by John Sparrow, 1648 (London: John M. Watkins, 1910, o.p.), VIII:1; p. 105.
15. *Aurora*, XVI:9; p. 411.
16. *Ibid.*, VIII:41; p. 155.
17. Cf. Sparrow translation, *Aurora*, XIII:106; p. 332. [TRANSLATOR'S NOTE: Sparrow's translation sometimes tones down any sexual imagery in Boehme. While the French translator Saint-Martin renders this passage with the French equivalent of "impregnates each other," Sparrow offers the rather pale "affects each other."]
18. Cf. Sparrow, *Aurora*, XXIII:45; pp. 622-623. [TRANSLATOR'S NOTE: Again the Sparrow translation is extremely circumspect: "For they wrestle in the birth or geniture *continually* one with another, like a loving play or scene."]

19. *Ibid.*, XXIII:18; pp. 615-616.
20. *Ibid.*, XIII: 88-88, 90-92; pp. 326-329. [TRANSLATOR'S NOTE: Because this is such a key passage in Boehme, and because the Sparrow translation quoted in the text is particularly abstruse in this case, we offer here an alternate version: "Suppose that there was before you a wheel made up of seven wheels, each enclosed inside another, so that each could go to either side, or in front of itself, or behind, or diagonally, without having to return; so that in its journey a wheel would always set another spinning but none would disappear; so that the turning of the seven wheels would maintain the movement of the central hub; so that all would remain visible and the hub would always move freely and would never wind down. . . . The seven wheels would be arranged inside of each other, like a globe. But one would always be able to see all seven at the same time, spinning separately, as well as the scale of the whole, with its rims, spokes, and hub; and the seven hubs in the middle would be like a single hub, which, as it turned, would move them all."]
21. See, for example, the excellent study by Ervin Laszlo, *Le Systémisme—vision nouvelle du monde* (Paris: Pergamon Press, 1981). [*The Systems View of the World* (New York: George Braziller, Inc., 1972).]
22. *Aurora*, XVI:12; p. 412.
23. Bernard d'Espagnat, *À la recherche du réel* (Paris: Gauthier-Villars, 1981), p. 26.
24. *Aurora*, XXI:105; p. 573.
25. Cf. Sparrow translation, *Aurora*, XVI:7; p. 410.
26. *Ibid.*, XIX:58; p. 499.
27. *Mysterium Magnum*, II:10; p. 6.
28. *Aurora*, XXIV:68; p. 655.
29. *Three Principles*, XVI: 5; p. 343.
30. *Ibid.*, IV:56; p. 55.
31. Basarab Nicolescu, *Nous, la particule et le monde*, Chapter Three.
32. *Ibid.*, Chapter Two.
33. James E. Lovelock, *Gaïa—A New Look at Life on Earth* (Oxford: Oxford University Press, 1982).
34. For a recent discussion of these epistemological developments, see the articles contained in *Lettre Science-Culture du Groupe de Réflexion Inter- et Transdisciplinaire*, No. 26 (June-July, 1987).
35. Gerald Holton, *L'Imagination scientifique* (Paris: Gallimard, 1981).
36. *Aurora*, III:53; p. 75.
37. Morin.
38. *Mysterium Magnum*, VIII:11; p. 42.
39. *Aurora*, XXV:68; p. 675.
40. *Ibid.*, XXIII:67; p. 627.
41. Alexandre Koyré, *La Philosophie de Jakob Boehme* (Paris: Vrin, 1971), p. 388.
42. *Mysterium Magnum*, VI:10; p. 31.
43. *Aurora*, XIX:26; p. 491.
44. Cf. Sparrow translation, *Aurora*, II:44; p. 58.
45. *Ibid.*, XIX:57; p. 499.

Send=Brieffe.

CHAPTER FOUR

The Imaginal as the Source of Reality

A: FALSE AND TRUE IMAGINATION

I N JACOB Boehme's cosmology, the interaction between the three-part structure of reality and its sevenfold organization is intimately linked to the active, dynamic role of the imagination. Like other traditional thinkers, Boehme introduces an essential distinction between a true, groundbreaking imagination (which has been called *imaginatio vera*) and a degenerate imagination which is destructive, divisive, devilish (mere *fantasy*). But the originality of Boehme's vision comes from his rigorous, precise approach to the concept of "imagination," obtained exactly from the relationship he introduces between it and the two laws governing every process of reality.

Indeed, this relationship has not eluded the analysts of Boehme's work. Thus, Pierre Deghaye stresses that each quality of the sevenfold cycle functions as a veritable fountain of the imagination: "Each degree of the sevenfold cycle represents one *quality* or *form*, and each one is destined to diversify itself infinitely. The seven *qualities* or *forms* are thus rather like *images* or *mirrors*."[1] But the consequences of this relationship have not been explored in a systematic way, in my opinion, because of the difficulties that have already been pointed out in understanding the *coherence* between the ternary and the septenary.

Thus most commentators on Boehme emphasize the primordial role of the divine imagination, which corresponds to the divine septenary. According to this interpretation, the divine imagination is the absolute matrix of all form, the starting point of all manifestation.

But this reverts to adopting a *linear* description of the sevenfold dynamic, contradicting Boehme's own texts, where he tells us constantly
that this linear description is an illusion created by ordinary language:
the inevitably linear, associative structure of natural language is
transposed at the level of the sevenfold dynamic.[2] In Boehme's cosmology, as I have said, all the septenaries have a cyclical non-linear
organization which permits the meshing of all the septenaries working
at different levels of reality, inside of each other. The divine imagination, considered just on the level of the divine septenary, would
produce only an illusory world, without consistency. Thus we see in
what sense "the Eternal, which is manifest in itself, manifests itself
also out of itself, and pours out its imagination."[3] It is precisely the
reciprocal "feeding" of all the septenaries which assures the consistency of innumerable forms and which engenders the extraordinary
diversity of different cosmoses. The divine septenary, considered
alone, separately from the other septenaries, certainly evokes for us
the purity of forms, that asymptotic and intangible purity of the
uncreated. The divine imagination gives us the illusion of pure and
permanent forms, in a closed world, where unity does not tolerate
diversity, where permanence does not tolerate impermanence. But
Boehme's whole cosmology is founded on the unity of contradictions.
Unity has meaning only through the existence of diversity, and diversity cannot be conceived without unity. Similarly, invariance nourishes itself on change, and what is fleeting would be absurd and
chaotic without invariance: "If a figure be imaged in a spirit, so that it
subsisteth; and if another spirit wrestleth with this, and gets the *better*,
then it comes to be divided, and indeed changed or altered, all according to the *kind* of the qualities; *and this is in God as a holy sport, play or
scene*."[4] True imagination is like a river of information which crosses
all levels of reality, assuring their coherence, their coexistence, their
non-separabilty. One could thus speak of veritable degrees of the
imagination, each corresponding to a certain level of reality. It is
these degrees all together which constitute true imagination, a world
in itself, where searchers have not lost touch with what Henry Corbin
calls *the imaginal world*.[5] This imaginal world is like a fabulous reser-
voir of data from which are drawn all the qualities of the sevenfold
cycle, which by their permanent struggle, transform the image into

embodiment. True imagination thus engenders reality, in a continual gushing forth, in a perpetual genesis. "The imagination," Deghaye writes, "is the faculty of producing images. The image in Boehme is not a pale imitation of a reality already perceived. It is itself a reality which elaborates itself and becomes perceptible for the first time. In German, *imagination* is *einbildung*. This substantive is formed partly by the verb *einbilden*, which perfectly reproduces the Latin *informare*: 'to give a form to, to fashion.' It is indeed in this primary sense that Boehme understands the act of imagining. For him, *imagination* is truly the creator of forms, that which models the substance and actualizes it."[6]

True imagination as the source of reality is a key idea in Boehme's cosmology. The recent translation of the Bible by André Chouraqui, written after a very long period of interdisciplinary research, reconfirms Boehme's vision in a rather unexpected way. The first word of Genesis, usually translated as "in the beginning," introduces from the outset the concept of time, in contradiction to the idea of timelessness characterizing eternity. Chouraqui's translation of this Hebrew word *Bereshit* is itself an extraordinary door to understanding the Biblical texts. "In fact the Hebrew word," Chouraqui writes, "does not signify 'In the beginning.' There are words to express this concept. Its meaning is a great deal more concrete. *Bereshit* is composed of three terms: *Be* (in), *Rosh* (head), and *it* (an ending which gives an abstract meaning to the word it concludes)."[7] It is thus, in a sense at once concrete and abstract, that Elohim created our own world *in his head*. In the same text on the first volume of the Bible it is written, "Elohim created man in his image/ in the image of Elohim created he him,"[8] and then, "YHWH Elohim fashions/ Man, Adam, the dust of the earth, Adamah."[9] There are thus two creations of man: one in the imagination, in form; the other, creaturely, out of the dust of the earth. It is indeed the true imagination which is the source of all reality.[10]

But, as I have already said, the universe of Jacob Boehme is not predetermined. In this self-organizing universe, each level of reality has its own freedom. The orientation of the sevenfold cycle is not fixed in advance. The sevenfold cycle can go forward or backward or even be interrupted by intervals of discontinuity. In particular, the whole process can stop at the end of the first triad of the sevenfold cycle, trapped in the dark world of the wheel of anguish. The imagination continues to act, but it becomes corrupted, it degenerates, it engenders hollow, unstable monsters. This *false imagination* has as much reality as the real imagination. It is "diabolical," in the etymological sense of the term: it *separates* and blocks the process of self-knowledge. Images generate other images, endlessly, in an infernal movement, where no image has any consistency. Matter is no longer engendered; nothingness feeds on nothingness. One sees why Boehme linked the false imagination to *vanity*. "For Nature would fain be delivered from this vanity, that it might procreate heavenly forms in the holy power."[11] "Vanity" and "the void" (in the sense of "nothingness") are intimately linked. Vanity, the void, and false imagination all represent active, powerful forces which are opposed to the accomplishment of the sevenfold cycle, to the birth of embodiment, of light. Do we not see them acting at every moment in our lives, every day? But we must not let ourselves fall into the trap of moral or psychological connotations. In Boehme's cosmology, as Miklos Veto has remarked, vanity "has a really metaphysical meaning."[12] Vanity is engendered by nonconformity, by a disrespect for its proper place in the cosmic processes. It is the false imagination which keeps it alive — that veritable *life of death*. But, paradoxically, the false imagination can have a constructive role. It is like a black light which allows us to see better the true light of life. Without the titanic cosmic struggle between the false and the true imagination, the sevenfold cycle could not be accomplished. Everything comes down to a question of *place*: the place of the false imagination is in the wheel of anguish, a necessary stage which must be passed beyond in order that there can be accomplishment. When this place is no longer respected, destruction, anarchy, and death establish themselves. In a world of false imagination, it is death which lives.

B: SLEEP AND THE IMAGINAL

Up until now we have used the word "imagination" in order to be true to the French translations of Jacob Boehme's writings and to the different commentaries published in French. But contemporary usage of the word "imagination" immediately makes one think of fancifulness, which is in total opposition to the meaning Boehme attributed to the word. That is why I prefer from now on, whenever possible, to use the phrase "the imaginal," one well established in modern terminology, especially since the writings of Gilbert Durand and his school.*

A discussion about the relationship between sleep and the imaginal would at first seem surprising. It is, however, crucial, for sleep appears in Boehme's writings as a central symbol in his cosmology, having a metaphysical meaning very different from the sense that the word evokes in everyday language.

"Behold and consider the sleep," Boehme writes, "and so you shall find it all. Sleep is nothing else but a being overcome."[13] But being overcome by whom, or what? This is precisely the process of the embodiment of the imaginal which contains the seed of sleep as an element of resistance, a blockage of that embodiment: "And then instantly the sun and stars wrestled with [Adam], and all the four elements wrestled so mightily and powerfully, that they overcame him; and [so] he sank down into a sleep."[14]

Sleep therefore seems like a stop, even like a break in the evolutionary process. It signifies the breaking of all contact with true imagination, a separation from the flow of reality by a turning back, a plunge into the abyss of the false imagination. Boehme speaks of "the Great Mystery of separability, out of which issued living beings."[15] This separability necessarily implies sleep as a stage of self-knowledge, a forgetting of the true nature. Sleep by itself is not harmful for "where sleep is, there the virtue [or power] of God is hidden in the centre."[16] But a sleep lasting an entire lifetime is equivalent to death. Thus Boehme, as a great teacher, constantly invites us to wake up. This resumption of contact with true imagination is a new birth. We can be

* TRANSLATOR'S NOTE: The French term "imaginaire" which Basarab Nicolescu uses at this point, is usually translated "the imaginary," which in English has the same wrong connotations of dreaminess and non-substantiality as the just-mentioned "imagination." In this translation, therefore, we have adopted the term popularized by Henry Corbin, "the imaginal," which Durand describes in The Encyclopedia of Religion as a way of presenting images of the higher, the ultimate, the divine without slipping into the trap of idolatry: it is clearly a creative imagination or inspiration of the highest order, whether the term is applied to metaphysics or (as Nicolescu and Durand both do) to physics.

reborn, in this life, by true imagination, by reestablishing our proper place in the movement of the universe that is non-separable from all levels of reality. Man builds himself by the power of true imagination; he is the incarnation of that imagination.

A surprising process of spiritual alchemy is described in Boehme's writings. For him, the imaginal and faith are inseparable. To the extent that each sevenfold cycle which leads to the embodiment of the imaginal corresponds to a certain degree of materiality, signifying that faith itself has a material consistency, it is a *food* which nourishes different levels of reality. The imaginal and faith on the human level thus nourish divinity by an ascending process, while the divine imaginal in turn nourishes man by a descending process, in a cycle perpetuated endlessly by those who believe. Boehme describes with no ambiguity *faith as nourishment*: "Christ, according to the eternal Word of the Deity, eateth not of the substance of heaven, as a creature, but of the human faith and earnest prayer, and the souls of men praising God, are his food. . . ."[17]

The reciprocal feeding of all levels of reality thus demands our active participation, through our opening the imaginal to true imagination. The sleep of man is thus equivalent to a veritable cosmic catastrophe: quite simply, it blocks the movement of the universe. This in no way signifies that the sleep of man and even his total disappearance as a species will impede the revolution of the planets or the existence of the galaxies. But the living universe of Jacob Boehme would then be transformed into a dead universe: mechanical, animated by a mere pretense of movement.

C: MODERN PHYSICS AND THE IMAGINAL WITHOUT IMAGES

A stubborn cliché holds that scientific inventiveness, especially in mathematics and theoretical physics, must be associated with a method of unshakable logic. It is true that a partial, technical scientific result generally arises out of the rigorous development of a kind of formalism. But in the great game of scientific invention, the ardent fire of the imaginal often plays a predominant role in relation to the imperturbable calm of scientific logic.

Important steps toward the comprehension of the role of the imaginal in modern mathematics have been taken in the testimonies of two great mathematicians: Henri Poincaré[18] and Jacques Hadamard.[19] In theoretical physics, the role of the imaginal has been explored by Gerald Holton.[20] I, too, have had occasion to express myself on the subject.[21]

Mathematics and theoretical physics are linked by a common characteristic: the imaginal here operates in an abstract, mathematical framework, whose subtlety and complexity preclude any quick understanding. But there is also an important difference between mathematics and theoretical physics: mathematicians are concerned about the internal coherence of their representations, while theoretical physicists, while sharing this concern, must also allow their representations to confront the fierce resistance of Nature. It is true that this difference is not as clear-cut as it first seems. After all, mathematical theories are engendered by the brain, and the brain has this extraordinary capacity of putting itself on an equal footing with Nature. This explains why certain mathematical theories have sometimes found their application in physics long after their discovery. It nonetheless happens that the direct presence of so-called "external" Nature introduces a new term into the dynamics of the imaginal in theoretical physics.

What interests us in the context of the present book is the emergence of a new form of the imaginal in quantum physics, characterized by the total abolition of image, at least of that which is founded on information furnished by the sense organs. This new form of the imaginal has been engendered by the confrontation between two different levels of reality; the macroscopic level (located at our own scale) and the quantum level.

I believe some examples may illustrate the sense of this proposal better than any theoretical development.

First of all, the scale at which one discovers the quantum world is, in and of itself, staggering. If one takes one centimeter and then cuts it into ten equal parts, and then takes one of those parts and also divides it into ten parts, and finally, continues this operation by carrying it out thirteen times (10^{-13} cm), one arrives at the threshold of the quantum world: an infinitely small oddity which, far from being simple, hides an infinite complexity. When we fathom even smaller distances, extraordinary surprises await us. For example, the unification of various interactions—strong, electromagnetic, and weak—takes place with a fabulous energy (10^{15} times greater than the energy corresponding to the mass of a proton). According to the law of Heisenberg, this energy corresponds to an infinitesimal distance (10^{-29} cm): if the proton was as large as the sun, this scale of unification would be that of a speck of dust (I leave to the reader the pleasure of discovering the corresponding proportion of his own body to this speck of dust). The unification of all these physical interactions takes place with an energy still more fabulous (10^{19} times the mass of a proton), which corresponds to an even tinier distance. How can we imagine the place where all the interactions fuse in one and the same interaction? How can the habitual imagination, based on information furnished by our sense organs, not feel dizzy contemplating such a scale? And still we must indeed resist this vertigo, if we do not wish our discourse on "reality" to transform itself into pure verbiage, into pure illusion. For this infinitesimal scale has a right to the status of "reality" as much as (if not more than) our own body does, or the objects which surround us in our everyday life.

In the quantum world the goddess "discontinuity" reigns. Energy varies by leaps and bounds: between two successive energy levels there is nothing—absolutely nothing, no other level of energy. The "quantum numbers" of particles (which are the characteristics of these particles, as our weight, the color of our eyes, etc., are the characteristics of our bodies) have precise, discrete values, and between two successive values of these quantum numbers, there is nothing—absolutely nothing, no other number possible. This discontinuity of which we speak is a true one—it has nothing in common with the meaning of the word in ordinary language (a fork in a road, for example). How can one imagine such a discontinuity? Let us try to imagine a "quantum ladder" where the steps are not *in any way* connected to each other, and try to imagine ourselves in the process of climbing such a ladder: an obviously impossible request—our habitual imagination instinctively fills in the gaps between the steps. Let us try another image: a bird jumping from one branch of a tree to another *without* passing through any intermediary point: it is as if the bird materialized suddenly on one branch or another. Evidently, our habitual imagination is blocked when confronting such a possibility, even if mathematics can treat this kind of situation rigorously.

Numerous other surprises await the voyager in this "Valley of Astonishment," in sharpening his sense of the imaginal, in forcing him to discover in himself an unsuspected degree of the imaginal which makes everything take its proper place. On his way, the traveler encounters one of these quantum particles which appears to him as a wave and a particle *at the same time.* "Contradiction, illusion!" he cries. "It is as if someone told me I am and I am not at the same time." But suddenly his face lights up, for he understands at last that it is his own way of seeing which, through a pattern conforming to his own nature, has discerned a wave *and* a particle at once: this inhabitant of he is, in fact, a good deal more complex than a wave or a particle.

More confident, he continues his voyage. And then he stops and can no longer accept what he sees. For he observes with his own eyes the famous quantum non-separability, of which he has often been told in works of popular science in his own world. He was ready to accept everything until now: that the inhabitants of this quantum world travel at dizzying speeds, incomparably greater than those of our rockets; that the emptiness which surrounds him is full of evanescent shapes which will appear and disappear continually, in a formal symphony of unequaled beauty; that the energy hidden in this quantum world is immense, with no measure common to the energies manifesting themselves in the traveler's own world. But this "non-separability" infuriates him. To see two inhabitants of this Valley of Astonishment, one located in one galaxy and the other in another galaxy, react simultaneously, like a single whole—that surpasses his capacity for accepting the unknown. How can these two particles react simultaneously when no known signal can link them together (our traveler indeed is well acquainted with the theory of relativity and knows that no signal can surpass the speed of light). "Magic, mystique, mystification!" he cries, determined to leave this quantum world, for he wants to save his reason at any price. And at this precise moment, he sees in front of him another traveler of his own world, a compatriot, who begins to talk to him. Surely there is something troubling about his face, first because this face vaguely reminds him of that of a sixteenth-century thinker, then because it suddenly resembles that of a twentieth-century physicist, and there are even moments when the face of the other traveler perfectly resembles his own. But his speech is serene, calm, reassuring, rational.

"There is nothing strange here," the second traveler tells him. "I have been here a long time and I've had the chance to convince myself of that. Rather, it is our own world which seems strange and incomprehensible to me now, and when we come back to it, we ought to make the necessary effort to understand it. Let us take this famous 'non-separability' which troubles you so much. An example could make you understand why there is nothing strange or magical about it. Imagine yourself again in your own familiar world, of three spatial dimensions. Now imagine a sheet of paper (of two spatial dimensions), peopled by all sorts of inhabitants whose sense organs allow them to perceive exactly what is happening in two dimensions, but only in two dimensions. Now, let us take a circle and let it gently penetrate the piece of paper, at a perpendicular angle. The inhabitants of this two-dimensional world will first of all see the sudden appearance of a dot. They will be convinced that this is a new phenomenon that should be studied with all their scientific means. Then they will see that the dot splits into two dots, which begin to move away from each other. They will make all sorts of experiments and will invent theories to explain completely what is going on. Complications begin when one of these two-dimensional physicists, among the most brilliant of his age, starts to point out with perfect clarity that the movement of the two dots demonstrates the existence of incomprehensible relationships: the two dots react as a solid whole, but there is no indication of their being linked together (according to the theory issued a long time ago among their experts, the physicists know that no signal can exceed a certain speed limit). The physicists of this two-dimensional world have just discovered 'non-separability.' The circle continues its movement, the two dots appearing on the sheet of paper, after having attained a maximal distance (the diameter of the circle), have again begun to approach each other until they join into one dot and then all trace of them suddenly disappears from the world of the piece of paper: the circle has quite simply passed through the sheet of paper and out the other side. During this time controversy has raged in the two-dimensional world, not only in the community of physicists, but also among philosophers and theologians. The general public from time to time has witnessed their televised debates or read some of their innumerable books and has understood nothing of what was going on. Up to the present day, non-separability is still considered a great mystery (even though a very powerful fellowship of those-who-think-well-according-to-their-own-sense-organs has tried to make them believe there is no mystery: one must read the mathematical equations, see that that's just how it works, and not try to 'understand' beyond these equations). However, *for us*, the situation is extremely simple and reasonable: it is only a circle passing through a piece of paper."

The face of the traveler again lights up. He understands that his own thinking habits impede the perception of a new reality.

He continues his journey for a long while and discovers many other marvels. After his trip (which would be too long to describe in detail here), he returns to his own world and writes a very learned book, *On the Nature of Space-Time*, which has extraordinary repercussions among his countrymen, not only among experts and philosophers, but also at all levels of society. As a result, many people now hurry to undertake the journey to the Valley of Astonishment, hoping secretly that they will at last be able to understand their own world, which meanwhile has become chaotic, anarchic, violent, crazy.

Of course, the journey we're talking about is an imaginary journey into the imaginal. No one has really "seen" quantum particles. Their properties are always detected in a very complex and indirect way by different measuring devices, especially by those modern-day cathedrals: giant particle-accelerators. Thus it is more and more difficult to separate experimental results from their theoretical interpretation: the theory becomes more and more an integral part of the "reality" of these particles. The situation is so complex that certain people prefer to deny any reference to such a "quantum reality": there is a group of operative prescriptions which work, that's all. Why try to imagine the unimaginable? One can recognize in this apparently rational position a strong dose of irrationality. Why close the eyes to the imaginal, unless we are afraid of losing our habitual way of thinking? Why close the doors to the imaginal, unless we are afraid of destroying the illusion (so strong in modern times) that *only one* level of reality

exists? This powerful metaphysical presumption lurks behind the
positions taken by so-called rationalists in a sort of rear-guard attack.

In fact, the imaginal of the quantum world opens up a fabulous
space for freedom, for comprehension, for dialogue, where reason is
not excluded but where, quite the contrary, it is what guides the steps
of the searcher for truth. It is truly a question of non-static evolutionary reason, which discovers its own successive steps in a continual
dialogue with Nature. Reason and the imaginal therefore cannot
really be dissociated. The imaginal helps us cross the threshold between different levels of reality, but it is reason which helps us to
explore a given level of reality rigorously.

In this context, I think that it is important to distinguish two types
of the imaginal in scientific inventiveness. The first form, the best-
known and the most common, corresponds to action inside only one
level of reality. A second form of the imaginal—which one might call
paradoxical—corresponds to action on *several* levels of reality. This
form, which manifests itself in the great inventiveness of new scientific
theories, is rarer and more subtle, more difficult to approach or test. It
is this form which is, in my opinion, similar to what is revealed in great
artistic creation.

If I were obliged to choose one name to incarnate the change in our
world view through quantum physics, I would without hesitation
choose Max Planck, the chief actor in this modern *Mahabharata*
which is playing itself out before our eyes in this century. The pages of
his *Scientific Autobiography* reveal all the complexity of his interior
process of clarification: "I have made vain attempts for a number of
years to adapt the elementary quantum of action in one way or another
to the framework of classical physics; these attempts have cost me a
great deal of effort. Many colleagues have found in this something that
bordered on tragedy. But I have a different opinion about it. For the
total enlightenment that I then experienced was for me an unequalled
enrichment. I knew with all certainty that the elementary quantum of
action played a much more important role in physics than I was
inclined to give it at first."[22]

The words "tragedy" and "total enlightenment" are worth remem-
bering. In what sense can one speak of a "tragedy" in connection with
a scientific idea? Is it linked to the obsessive illusion of a *single* level of

reality? And what exactly is the nature of this "total enlightenment" experienced by Planck? Is it linked to an acceptance of the existence of *several* levels of reality?

The confrontation between two different levels of reality through the action of the imaginal contains within itself an immense potential for revealing the poetic content of the universe, for the reenchantment of the world. It is not a question, obviously, of more or less arbitrary lyrical effusions, inspired by a superficial contemplation of the "marvels" of modern science, but rather one of a more whole engagement of the human being on the road to self-knowledge and knowledge of the universe. The "well-informed" imaginal can incorporate mathematical abstraction as well as freedom of intuition, the data obtained from the exploration of Nature as well as the feelings awakened by the contemplation of these data. It is this "well-informed" imaginal which today allows the opening of a major dialogue between science, art, and Tradition.

NOTES

1. Pierre Deghaye, *La Naissance de Dieu ou La doctrine de Jakob Boehme* (Paris: Albin Michel, Collection *Spiritualités Vivantes*, 1985) p. 257.
2. This remark recalls in a striking manner the difficulties we have in translating quantum physics into the terminology of classical physics—difficulties forcefully stressed by the founding fathers of quantum mechanics, in particular Niels Bohr.
3. Jacob Boehme, *Sex Puncta Theosophica or High and Deep Grounding of Six Theosophic Points: An Open Gate to All the Secrets of Life Wherein the Causes of All Being Become Known*, written in the year 1620. Translated into English by John Rolleston Earle as part of *Six Theosophic Points and Other Writings* (New York: Alfred A. Knopf, 1920, o.p.), II:19; p. 36.
4. *The Aurora*, translated into English by John Sparrow, original edition published in 1656. (London: John M. Watkins, 1960, o.p.), XII:172; p. 307.
5. Jean-Louis Vieillard-Baron, "Le Problème du dualisme dans la pensée de Jakob Boehme," in *Jakob Boehme*, proceedings of a colloquium organized by the Centre d'Études et de Recherches Interdisciplinaires de Chantilly (C.E.R.I.C.), (Paris: Vrin, 1979), p. 68.
6. Pierre Deghaye, "Psychologia Sacra," in *Jakob Boehme* (Paris: Albin Michel, Collection *Cahiers de l'Hermétisme*, 1977), p. 220.
7. *La Bible*, translated into French and presented by André Chouraqui, vol. *Entête*, (Paris: Desclée, De Brouwer et Cie., 1979), p. xi; to keep the multitude of meanings attributed over the last two thousand years to the word, *"Bereshit,"* Chouraqui adopts the neologism, *"Entête."*
8. *Ibid.*, p. 17.
9. *Ibid.*, p. 18.
10. A detailed comparison of the biblical texts, in their translation by André Chouraqui, to texts by Jacob Boehme would lead, I am convinced, to the discovery of surprising corre-

spondences, unknown up to now, but such a comparison far surpasses my own competence.

11. *Aurora*, IV:46; p. 96.

12. Miklos Veto, "Le Mal selon Boehme," in *Jakob Boehme*, C.E.R.I.C. colloquium notes, p. 107.

13. Jacob Boehme, *Concerning the Three Principles of the Divine Essence*, translated by John Sparrow, 1648 (London: John M. Watkins, 1910, o.p.), XII:18; p. 204.

14. *Ibid.*, XII:16; p. 203.

15. Jacob Boehme, *De l'élection de la grace*, translated into French by Debeo (Milan: Arché, 1976), p. 95.

16. *Three Principles*, XVII:28; p. 379.

17. *Mysterium Magnum*, translated by John Sparrow, 1654 (London: John M. Watkins, 1924, o.p.), LXX:60; p. 822.

18. Henri Poincaré, Bulletin de l'Institut Géneral de Psychologie, no. 3, 1908; the text of this conference was reprinted in *Science et méthode*, Chapter 3, "L'Invention mathématique," (Paris: Flammarion, 1908).

19. Jacques Hadamard, *Essai sur la psychologie de l'invention dans le domaine mathématique*, in the collection "Discours de la méthode," (Paris: Gauthier-Villars, 1978); the first edition of this book was published in 1945, in English, by Princeton University Press, Princeton, N.J.

20. Gerald Holton, *The Scientific Imagination: Case Studies* (New York: Cambridge University Press, 1978); *Thematic Origin of Scientific Thought: Kepler to Einstein* (Cambridge: Harvard University Press, 1973).

21. Basarab Nicolescu, Chapter 5 of *Nous, la particule et le monde* (Paris: Le Mail, 1985); also, see "L'imaginaire sans images: symboles et thêmata dans la physique contemporaine," in *Cahiers de l'Imaginaire*, no. 1: "L'Imaginaire dans les sciences et les arts" (Toulouse: Editions Privat, 1988), pp. 25-36; and "Vision de la réalité et réalité de la vision: l'imaginaire dans la physique moderne," in *IRIS*, the review of the Centre de Recherche sur l'Imaginaire de Grenoble, no. 2, 4th quarter, 1986, pp. 35-57.

22. Max Planck, *Autobiographie scientifique*, translated and with preface and notes by André George (Paris: Albin Michel, 1960), p. 64. [English translation: *Scientific Autobiography and Other Papers*, translated by Frank Gaynor (Westport, Conn.: Greenwood Press, 1968), reprint of 1949 edition.]

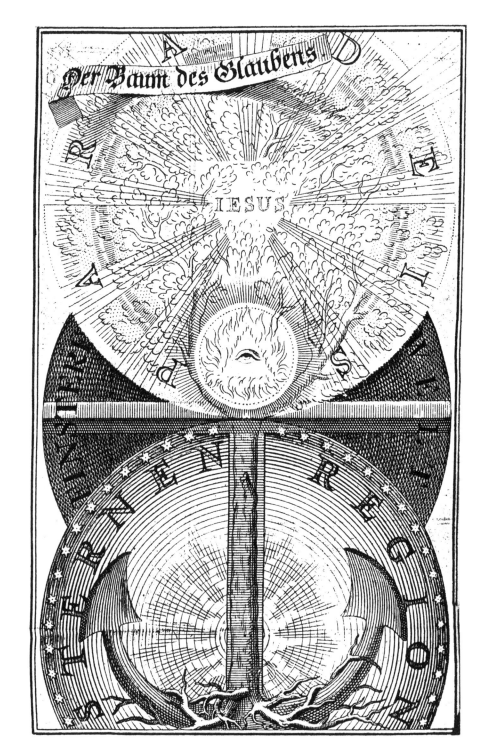

CHAPTER FIVE

Unexpected Encounter: Science and Tradition

A: NECESSARY DISTINCTIONS: THE WORDS "SCIENCE" AND "TRADITION"

HE contemporary encounter between science and tradition is indeed a fertile ground for multiple confusions. Activated by the changes which fundamental science (and especially quantum physics) has made in logic, in epistemology, and in our view of the world, this subject has even become fashionable: numerous books (some of which are best sellers) and numerous colloquiums try, for better or worse, to clarify the ties between modern scientific thought and traditional thought. What is at first surprising about this debate is the competence (or rather the incompetence) of most of the participants. Non-scientists are seen expressing themselves cheerfully on complex problems of quantum physics (complex even for specialists), and writers who plainly know practically nothing about tradition hold forth with total assurance on any subject whatever relating to traditional thought. The situation becomes even more ludicrous (or even more disturbing) when the same writers disclose to us the links or the absence of links between science and tradition. For everything, or almost everything, seems to have been already asserted in this domain, ranging, on one hand, from the proclamation of the sameness of the world views proposed by tradition (especially Far Eastern traditions) and science, to the opposite extreme, proclaiming the absence of any bridge whatsoever between them. But, of course, this kind of research cannot be undertaken by proclamation; militant passions can only obscure the debate.

Two facts need to be stressed clearly, it seems to me.

On the one hand, the present debate, unimaginable at the start of the century in the epoch of triumphant scientism, has the merit of revealing the existence of a real problem in spite of all the inherent or intentional confusions. After all, fundamental science has its roots in the compost of questions common to all realms of knowledge: What is the meaning of life? What is the role of man in the cosmic process? What is the place of nature in knowledge? Gradually, indeed, these questions have come to be considered non-scientific and have been banished to the limbo of irrationality, the domain reserved for the poet, the mystic, the artist, or the philosopher. But science is a continuing process, and one wonders if it has not returned on its own to its sources, a return enriched by all it has acquired through the scientific methodology which it has had at its disposal throughout history.

On the other hand, the innumerable confusions which have been manifested by this debate are at least partly inevitable. Both modern science and tradition are regions of extraordinary complexity. It is difficult, if not impossible, for one and the same person to command at the same time *the knowledge and the practice* of both domains. In my opinion, the search for links between modern science and tradition is a preeminently transdisciplinary problem: it requires the coming together of the very best experts in both fields to advance this research. That does not mean that in the absence of truly transdisciplinary research, all individual opinion is banished. Dialogue remains possible on the condition that each speaker stays within his own field of expertise. At any rate, that is the attitude I myself adopt.

One other aspect in particular seems to complicate this debate: the question of the meaning of the word "tradition" itself.

First of all there is the general usage which makes one think immediately of "custom," "habits," or "manner of thinking, doing, or acting, which is a heritage of the past."[1] Of course, that is not the connotation which is adopted in the science-tradition debate, but it could insidiously confuse an uninformed public. Even journals and reviews of a high intellectual quality carefully avoid addressing the debate between science and tradition for fear that their readers might associate it with right-wing political connotations; for is it not true that "tradition" is supposed to be a privilege of the right wing? This situation might seem cartoon-like, but unfortunately it corresponds to a sad reality.

There is a second meaning of the term which is less current, but it is the only one adapted to our context, in which "tradition" refers to "the whole of beliefs and practices, religious or moral, transmitted from century to century, originally by word or example" and also "the whole of knowledge, more or less legendary, related to the past, transmitted at first orally from generation to generation."[2] According to this definition, Tradition encompasses different "traditions"—Christian, Jewish, Islamic, Buddhist, Sufi, etc. To avoid the first usage of the word "tradition," one often writes it with a capital T.

But even this second usage of the word "tradition" gives rise to confusion. In a fundamental study of Western esoterism,[3] Antoine Faivre suggests a triple distinction which can help us eliminate possible ambiguity. He thus distinguishes three contemporary lines of Tradition: the *severe* or *purist* line, the *historical* line, and the *humanist* or *alchemical* line. "The representatives of the 'purist' line," Faivre writes, "pose the existence of a 'primordial' Tradition—which should not be taken in a historical or chronological sense—of a 'non-human origin,' as was often said by René Guénon, indisputably the master of this line of thought in the twentieth century. A deposit of wisdom and gnostic thought used to belong to humanity, which has let it scatter and dissolve."[4] As for the "historical" line, it emphasizes "the ways of emergence through *the* traditions. . . . The champions of the second line glean freely here and there, according to a process comparable to what students in the United States call 'shopping around': in the first year of college they enroll in various courses, often vastly different from each other, before choosing their major."[5] Finally, there is the "humanist" line, which is open to modern times: "with the third line, it is a matter of taking the world as primary material, the whole world that Guénon scorns as the product of the Kali Yuga."[6] Nature, culture, and science are not rejected by the third line. It goes without saying that it is this third approach to Tradition, of which Jacob Boehme is an illustrious precursor, that interests us in the context of an encounter between Tradition and modern science.

The expression "modern science" is somewhat less ambiguous, but

it also gives rise to various confusions. "Scientific method" is confounded with "scientific theory" and "scientific theory" with interpretation of one scientific theory, not to mention the confusion so current
(and so pernicious) between "science" and "scientism" or between
"fundamental science" and "technology." It is impossible to clarify all
these confusions here, but some necessary distinctions need to be
introduced.

First of all, is it legitimate to speak of "science," or must one instead
speak of "sciences" (just as certain people question whether we should
speak of "Tradition" or "traditions")? What we see displayed in actual
scientific activity is something like an explosion of a multitude of
sciences, of an extraordinary variety, each having an almost absolute
autonomy in its own field. Certainly the area of overlap between the
different sciences is not a void, and the undisputed value of interdisciplinary studies is due to this fact. The frontier discovered between two different sciences is often an area of great fertility. It is
exactly at these frontiers that new sciences are born: new sciences
which in their turn acquire an almost absolute autonomy. But the
existence of these frontiers, these overlapping areas between different
sciences, does not assure the unity of science: it simply demonstrates
the value of certain methods which, while engendering new sciences,
nevertheless do not have a universal character.

Well, then, has science a unity? The unicity of scientific method
does not patently signify the unity of science. If this unity exists, it
must be searched for elsewhere. In this context, Gerald Holton's proposition is seductive.[7] Holton demonstrated the existence of hidden
but stable structures in the evolution of scientific ideas: *thêmata*.
These are ontological presuppositions, unconscious for the most part
(they do not appear in the organized body of science), but which
dominate the thinking of scientists. They generally present themselves as double or triple alternatives: evolution—involution; continuity—discontinuity;   simplicity—complexity;   invariance—
variation; holism—reductionism; unity—hierarchical structure;
constancy—change, etc. Two characteristics strike those who study
these thêmata: (1) their antiquity and persistence through time; and
(2) their limited number: Holton counts only a few score of these
thêmata in the whole history of science. He thus could affirm that "it is

this durability of a relatively small number of thêmata, as well as their diffusion at a given moment throughout the whole community, that has given science the permanent identity that it preserves, in a certain measure, in spite of the developments and changes that take place in it."[8] This proposition of the unity of science is justified, and we can adopt it as a good working hypothesis.

Once this distinction between "science" and "the sciences" is made, we can quite quickly come to grips with other necessary distinctions.

Scientific method is unique and invariable: it has not changed since the works of Galileo and other founders of modern science. That does not mean that this scientific method might not change someday; but this change could take place only under the pressure of the absolute necessity to include experimental data and not on the say-so of some scientist or philosopher. Although scientific method has not changed for several centuries, on the other hand *scientific theory* is characterized by perpetual change. There has never been, nor will there ever be, an immutable theory: each theory has only a limited area of validity and it is necessarily overturned by certain experimental data. The unknown is inexhaustible; Nature is inexhaustible. One could even affirm that the greatness of science resides precisely in the perpetual change of scientific theories. At a naive glance, this change can seem like a failure. One hears here or there voices designating this change as a proof of science's fragility, of its inadaptability to knowledge. But what would it mean to have a "final theory," inflexible and unchangeable? Quite simply, the death of knowledge. The desire for a "final theory" is only the product of hallucination.

Other distinctions should be made before approaching the problem of the relationship between science and Tradition.

A *scientific theory* has its own language, its own methods, its own internal coherence and it is more or less mathematically formalized. Thanks to this, a scientific theory arrives at certain results. The *interpretation* of these results on an ontological level momentarily escapes the boundaries of science for a moment for it brings into play another language, other methods, another internal coherence. The confusion between a scientific theory and its interpretation on the ontological level can lead to even worse confusions. The introduction of ontology into science will perhaps be the source of a great scientific revolution in the future, but for the moment this revolution has not taken place.

Another pernicious confusion is that which exists between science and "scientism." Modern science (at least in the spirit of its founders and also in that of the majority of contemporary scientists) obviously does not have the means to claim to be the sole path to knowledge and truth. Its own methodology imposes upon it certain inevitable limits. For example, the repeatability of scientific findings is an essential part of the methodology of modern science. But reality and our own lives are also characterized by singular events, by non-repeatable occurrences. Modern science is not concerned with singular events, and therefore there is a whole realm of reality which escapes it completely. But, in spite of everything, *scientism*, an ideology born of the phantasm of the absolute power of man over nature and over himself, claims that science and reason are the only paths to knowledge and truth: science alone, reason alone. This hallucination has been productive and, after all, positive for a given epoch, for it has led to extraordinary scientific advances. But today it is becoming a formidable restraint, for it is in opposition to science's real development. But although scientism is dying, it is not completely dead, though its disappearance seems to me inevitable. Paradoxically, the progressive disappearance of scientism in the exact sciences has been accompanied by its reinforcement in the human sciences (perhaps because they try to imitate a science that is now outdated—that of the nineteenth century). This paradoxical process explains, at least partially, the tenacious persistence of the confusion between science and scientism.

Finally, one must distinguish between *fundamental science* and *technology*. In the eyes of the general public (but also of certain philosophers, sociologists, and politicians), interplanetary rockets and the atomic bomb *are* fundamental science, instead of being the *results* of fundamental science. Technology is the bastard daughter of fundamental science: she has one foot in knowledge and one foot elsewhere. In our time, certainly, the demarcation between fundamental science and technology is more and more difficult to distinguish, to the extent that fundamental science is called upon to solve technological problems. But that is a question of a local and partial phenomenon. Fundamental science remains globally concerned about the confrontation with the unknown, without a precise aim.

This long digression on the words "science" and "Tradition" was inevitable if we are to rigorously approach the relationship between the two realms of knowledge designated by these words.

B: SCIENCE AND TRADITION:
IMPASSABLE BARRIER OR INTERACTION?

An impassable barrier seems to separate science and Tradition.

In my book, *Nous, la particule et le monde,* I have analyzed at length the differences between science and Tradition. Let me recall here a few of those differences: "Traditional knowledge is based on revelation, on contemplation, on the direct perception of reality. At the opposite pole, scientific knowledge . . . is based on the understanding of reality by the intermediary of the mind alone, through logical and mathematical constructions. . . . Traditional research accords a great importance to the body, to sensations, to the feelings, to faith, while scientific research excludes the searcher's own body, his sensations, his feelings, his faith from the field of observation and the formulation of 'laws' . . . Traditional thought has always affirmed that reality is not linked to time and space: it *is* . . . At the opposite pole, the scientific searcher is obliged to postulate the existence of an 'objective' reality that is separated from and independent of all observation or measure and which is strongly defined in space and in time . . . Traditional research demands the right to an experience incommunicable by ordinary language: The traditional experience is unique, total, far surpassing the categories of ordinary logic. In contrast, scientific experiment is communicable and can be repeated. . . . Traditional knowledge demands *the right to inefficacy* on the plane of material space and time, on the plane of directly observable materiality. . . . On the other hand, science interests itself essentially in the 'external body,' in the maximum efficacy on the plane of direct materiality."[9]

The fact that traditional knowledge and scientific knowledge can be present in one and the same person by no means demonstrates the existence of some kind of bridge between science and Tradition. For example, one can be at the same time a practitioner of the Kabbalah and a brilliant biologist and still refuse to recognize any link whatsoever between the Kabbalah and biology. Or one can be a fervent Christian and a great specialist in quantum physics and deny that there is any relationship whatsoever between religion and physics.

The teaching of Jacob Boehme, with his theory of the double nature of Nature, provides us with the possibility of a rigorous approach to the much-discussed question about the relationship between science and Tradition. At the same time, this approach opens us to astonishing perspectives which I am convinced will stimulate completely unexpected developments in very diverse areas of contemporary life. If we accept the idea of a sevenfold dynamic at work in each process of reality, we are led inexorably to the conclusion that fundamental science, such as that practiced today, is concerned only with the *three first qualities* of the sevenfold cycle. Stated a different way, modern science finds itself firmly trapped in the "wheel of anguish."

The three first qualities of the sevenfold cycle are those closest to the magical source of reality. But at the same time, they are the *furthest* from realization, from the successful completion of the cycle.

The context I am proposing allows us to shed light simultaneously on the essential difference between science and Tradition and their equally essential relationship.

It is the very methodology of modern science which places it in the first triad of the sevenfold cycle, where the destiny of the whole cosmic drama is played out, in an unrestrained desire for manifestation, in a tumultuous dynamic that wants to go out toward joy, toward love, toward spiritual accomplishment. Modern science is like an extremely finely-tuned and exact probing device which permits us a glimpse of that "wheel of anguish." But scientific methodology, which is the fundamental condition for the success and the efficacy of science, at the same time limits the scope of this probing device. Thus one sees the deep-rooted motivation (perhaps unconscious) of the wish to eliminate the subject in the natural sciences, a wish that guided the steps of the founders of modern science. Science has brought about these rapid advances at the cost of separating the subject from Nature, which is perceived as an object of study. This is a principal difference between science and Tradition, which in various ways has always stressed the unity of all that exists, a unity in diversity, indeed, but which cannot exclude joy, love, spiritual development, the human being and the whole cosmos. In the light of Jacob Boehme's philosophy, one could say that Tradition is concerned with the totality of the sevenfold cycle and with the interaction among all the sevenfold cycles acting in all the different cosmoses.

One can thus understand the deep-seated origin of *scientism* and its lack of metaphysical scope. Scientism consists of taking the first triad of the sevenfold cycle as an absolute, elevated as the one and only reality. The very existence of the other four qualities of the sevenfold cycle is denied. As a result, the interaction among different sevenfold cycles is itself reduced to nothing. There is thus only one level of reality, a horizontal level opposing all verticality. The verticality extolled by scientism is a false verticality, a simple optical illusion, since movement can take place only in one dimension—that of the "wheel of anguish." This wheel is no longer a stage of movement; it *is* the movement. It becomes the wheel of anguish in the full meaning of the term. Everything goes around in circles (which could be a good definition of hell); everything becomes justified: totalitarianism, violence, destruction of others in the name of good principles. And, in the end, there is only one way out: self-destruction. Scientism is not only an ideology; it is truly a religion, a religion without God. Scientism, with all its philosophical and sociological ramifications, unknowingly repeats the action of Lucifer who, looking behind himself at the magical source of reality, wants to possess it, but is ignorant of the fact that this action means his own ruin.

It is not hard to understand all the confusion which dominates the thought of certain contemporary Traditionalists who deny (always of course in different words) the existence of the three first qualities of the sevenfold cycle. This current of thought is the exact mirror image of scientism, even though it presents itself as scientism's relentless enemy. It mistakes the part for the whole, making exactly the same error as that of scientism. The value of science is denied completely: science is thrown into outer darkness, that of impure, dead "matter," cut off completely from the soul, the spirit, the sacred, the divine. This seemingly angelic attitude fails in the end by the same action as Lucifer's: that of perpetuating forever the "wheel of anguish."

There is furthermore an intermediate attitude between the militant scientists and the militant Traditionalists—that of those who see "spirit" everywhere, in particles, in genes, in planets or stars. The sevenfold cycle is not denied, but it is reduced in fact to one solitary quality. These people see joy, love, soul, spirit, and who knows what, strolling everywhere, in a confusion that is perhaps sympathetic and reassuring, but which engenders all sorts of possible driftings off-course.

Does the essential difference between science and Tradition mean that there is no bridge at all between these two realms of knowledge?

Another response, for the moment purely speculative, is furnished by the context I am proposing. If science is situated in the first triad of the sevenfold cycle and Tradition is concerned with the whole cycle, their relationship is clear: science and Tradition make no sense without each other. To reduce the sevenfold cycle to this first triad means the cessation of movement, a self-destructive reality. On the other hand, to rob the cycle of the knowledge of the first triad means making its continuing movement, or a true accomplishment of the cycle, impossible.

But the response that I have just outlined will be speculative and disembodied if it is not based on concrete scientific development.

I wish only to come to grips with some major facts here, the detailed analysis of which it is impossible to make except by transdisciplinary research, as I have clearly underlined before. It goes without saying that, in this approach, I shall not question scientific *theories*, in their formal or mathematical aspects, for they are, by definition, silent on the ontological level. The points of contact between science and Tradition can be found only in the fundamental scientific axioms or the most general results obtained by science. In other words, it is the *interpretation* of scientific theories that I shall question, an interpretation which thus becomes more and more inseparable from scientific theory itself.

The emergence in this century of quantum physics, with its discovery of a level of reality different from the macrophysical, constitutes one of these major facts, with consequences we have not finished exploring, on all the planes of our life. In the Boehmian context, this signifies the *interaction* between the sevenfold cycles located at different levels of reality, an interaction which takes place through the relationship among the first triads at different levels. Even if there is a split between the quantum level and the macrophysical level (through the different laws which govern the two), there is at the same time continuity: the one cannot exist without the other. The proof: our own existence and that of our universe. The discovery of a level of reality different from our own brings our very selves into play: we are those who obligatorily must make the translation from one level to the other. A sense of verticality thus begins to make itself felt on the plane of language if not of understanding. At the same time, there appears to be a movement from the quantum level towards the macrophysical level. Our visible macrophysical world is built on the invisible quantum world. Our world thus appears, in a sense, as the invisible made visible.

The logic which rules the quantum world is different from that which rules our own world. All the writings of Lupasco testify to the richness of this logic of contradictories in its philosophical implications. But what interests me here is the kinship between quantum logic and traditional thought. The thêmata of the quantum world, as alternatives to contradictions, appear to be outmoded and replaced by a veritable unity of contradictories: something not continuous *or* discontinuous, but continuous *and* discontinuous; not simplicity or complexity, but simplicity and complexity; not unity or hierarchical structure, but unity and hierarchical structure; not constancy or change, but constancy and change. The quantum entity is at the same time continuous and discontinuous. The physical interactions appear at once unified and structured hierarchically, according to the scale of energy on which they are being explored. The quantum world seems at once simple (through its fundamental laws which ensure the unity of interactions) and extremely complex (through the infinite variety of phenomena at different energy levels). Quantum entities ask at the same time for symmetry and a break in this symmetry. The thêmata appear thus at most like facets of a symbol. I have discussed elsewhere[10] some idea-symbols of modern physics. The reconciliation between contemporary scientific thought and traditional symbolic thought is a major encounter which is the sign, I think, of a still more important encounter: that between the world explored by Tradition and the world explored by science. What Tradition discovers in the richness of the interior life, science discovers, by correspondence, in the corporeality of natural systems.

Is the unification of all physical interactions the corresponding sign of an even more profound unification, that which is spoken of as Tradition? Is the fascinating coherence between the infinitely small and the infinitely large a sign corresponding to an even still more profound coherence, between all the levels of reality described by Tradition? These are dizzying questions, to which it would be premature to outline a response, but their formulation is inevitable.

Finally, why does the unification of all physical interactions require a multidimensional space-time so different from our own? What is signified by the extremely rapid rolling-up of supplementary dimensions into an infinitesimal region of space? There is a great temptation to characterize the different levels of reality of which Tradition tells us by a space-time with a larger and larger number of dimensions (does God live in a space-time with an infinite number of dimensions?), but I cannot take this step, for it seems to me to lead to an abusive simplification, one of extreme intellectual and spiritual poverty, in opposition to the teaching of Tradition. This temptation, as fascinating as it might be, has as its source the same error as that which I stressed before: reducing the sevenfold cycle to its first triad. In which space-time is love located? An absurd question which is not, paradoxically, the prerogative of scientists only.

In a celebrated book written a century ago, Edwin Abbott[11] described the adventures of a two-dimensional being who was snatched from his own world by a three-dimensional being. In his marvel at discovering a world infinitely richer than his own, he believes that the three-dimensional being is a god. But he realizes progressively that this marvelous world, like his own world, is peopled by criminals and wise men, by poets and hoodlums, by the good and the wicked. Are they gods? Certainly not. But this conclusion does not prevent our two-dimensional being from returning to his own world and proclaiming, at the risk of his own life, that there are other worlds, other realities.

According to the context we propose, based on the writings of Jacob Boehme, the value of dialogue between modern science and

Tradition is not found in an abusive identification of the results of science with certain affirmations of traditional thought. After an interesting colloquium at Sainte-Baume on the theme of "Alliance," André Chouraqui wrote to me: "Without the transcendence of unity and of love, the universe would be incomprehensible, whereas each day it becomes, incomprehensibly, more comprehensible."[12] Tradition is nourished by science, by time, by history, while science obtains all its meaning (and, in particular, its sense of values) by interacting with Tradition.

NOTES

1. See, for example, Le Petit Robert, the alphabetical and analogic dictionary of the French language, by Paul Robert (Paris: S.N.L., 1970), p. 1810.
2. Ibid.
3. Antoine Faivre, Accès de l'ésotérisme occidental (Paris: Gallimard, Bibliothèque des Sciences Humains, 1986), especially the chapter "Définitions et positions," pp. 13-50.
4. Ibid., p. 34.
5. Ibid., p. 36.
6. Ibid., p. 38.
7. Gerald Holton, L'Imagination scientifique (Paris: Gallimard, 1981); Thematic Origin of Scientific Thought: Kepler to Einstein (Boston: Harvard University Press, 1973); The Scientific Imagination: Case Studies (New York: Cambridge University Press, 1978).
8. Holton, "Les Thêmata dans la pensée scientifique," in L'imagination scientifique, p. 30.
9. Basarab Nicolescu, Nous, la particule et le monde (Paris: Le Mail, 1985) p. 159-161.
10. Ibid.
11. Edwin A. Abbott, Flatland (New York: New American Library, 1984).
12. André Chouraqui, letter to the author, dated July 7, 1987.

Der Weg zu Christ

Matth: 11 & 12

Ioël. 2.   ζ. 12. 13.

CHAPTER SIX

Jacob Boehme and the Evolution of Man

LUCIFER'S ACTION: CONTEMPORARY RESONANCES

I T IS well known that Boehme's doctrine of good and evil is one of the most important parts of his work. It would be presumptuous on my part to analyze it here after so many erudite studies have been made. I limit myself to the aspects linked to the formulation of a future Philosophy of Nature that would be suitable for our era.

As I have stressed time and again, Boehme's thought is based on a logic of contradictories, as one of his essential ideas is *the unity of opposites*. God himself is the incarnation of this unity of opposites: "For the God of the holy world, and the God of the dark world, are not two Gods; there is but one only God: he himself is all being, essence, or substance; he is evil and good, heaven and hell, light and darkness, eternity and time, beginning and end."[1]

The unity of all the sevenfold cycles is truly beyond good and evil. Good and evil appear when there is a dysfunction in a sevenfold cycle or in the interaction between the different sevenfold cycles. Therefore there is a quite logical, clear definition of "evil" as anything which is opposed to the development of a sevenfold cycle or the interaction between these different cycles. In other words, evil is anything which opposes the birth of God. Unquestionable signs of evil are the complete taking over of the cycle by one or several of the qualities in it, the stopping of the cycle, or, once again, the change of direction of the sequence of the cycle.

Evil has a positive side so long as it is a resistance to the develop-

ment of the cycle, a resistance which conditions the movement. Without this resistance everything would be devoured by the incomparable
fire at the magical source of reality; it is a protection against this
consuming fire. This is why "there is nothing in nature wherein there
is not good and evil; everything moveth and liveth in this double
impulse."[2] Good and evil appear as two qualities "which are in each
other as one thing in this world, in all powers, in the stars and the
elements, as also in all the creatures. . . ."[3] Even "the kingdom of
God and the kingdom of hell hang one to the other, as *one* body, and
yet the one cannot comprehend the other."[4] "Hell" is the first triad of
the sevenfold cycle. If it respects its function, which is that of being, in
Boehme's language, "the flame of anger," the movement can proceed
for "the flame of anger is the manifestation of the great love."[5] The
anger is "the root of life," but "if it be without the light, then it is not
God, but hell fire."[6]

Evil transforms itself into an ontological catastrophe when it
changes function: resistance turns into complete opposition in relation to the development of the sevenfold cycle and the interaction
between the different cycles. The order of the world is turned upside-
down. Harmony becomes chaos, and constructive interaction is replaced by an anarchic, self-destructive movement. In particular,
"hell" becomes truly infernal: the first triad closes up on itself in a
world of darkness, shutting itself off from any penetration by the light.

Evil is therefore a quality of being which is neither positive nor
negative. But it is equivalent to an ontological catastrophe when it
changes function. At our level of reality, the freedom of man comes at
the price of a difficult, trying choice, where the will of man plays a
crucial role.

The catastrophe is symbolized in a magnificent way by the fall of
Lucifer, which occupies such a significant place in the work of Jacob
Boehme. "Lucifer was born in the beginning as a being of light,"
Pierre Deghaye writes. "He is the output of a sevenfold emanation
which begins in the darkness and completes itself in the light. His
regression inverts the course of this process. . . . The violence done to
nature destroys the divine manifestation. It abolishes the birth of
God. It is a *deicidal* violence."[7]

What was Lucifer's crime, basically? That of looking backwards, toward the magical source of reality, "but he became a fool; therefore *this place* or space, in its burning quality, could *not* subsist in God, whereupon the creation of this world ensued."[8]

By this backward glance, Lucifer reverses the direction of the seven-fold cycle. This change of direction is not made innocently, for each quality of the sevenfold cycle is transformed into its own opposite. Lucifer is the creator of the upside-down sevenfold cycle, which en-genders "the house of darkness," the house of death. Jacob Boehme gives us a striking description of this upside-down cycle in *The Aurora*: "Here is lamentation and woe, *yelling* and crying, and no deliverance; it is with them as if it did *continually* thunder and lighten tem-pestuously. For the kindled spirits of God generate themselves thus. . . . The fire *burneth* as a fierce wrathful Sulphur. . . . Love is an *enmity* here. . . . The sound is a mere beating, *rumbling* or crack-ing. . . . The circuit, region, court or *residence* of the body of the seven is a house of *mourning*. Their food is *abomination*, and groweth from the fierceness of all qualities."[9] It is death which lives in the world of this upside-down cycle, a world where the king is Lucifer turned into Satan.

The completion of this reversed cycle is the first triad, that of the wrath of God, that which Boehme calls "the outermost birth in *this* world,"[10] that of the wheel of anguish, that of the "natural fire, which is a torment and consuming source."[11]

The idea of the danger of the backward glance runs through texts of all times. The wife of Lot, Abraham's nephew, is turned into a pillar of salt for having looked back during the destruction of Sodom. Orpheus descends to hell to bring back Eurydice, but, not keeping his promise, he turns to look at her and she disappears into the darkness.

Let us look around ourselves, in our own world today, and dare to pose to ourselves this question: Are we on the verge of repeating this action by Lucifer, this backward glance? Are we on the verge of forever locking ourselves inside the wheel of anguish? A philosopher of the stature of Michel Henry is not afraid to write: "It is life itself which is wounded; all its values are wavering, not only aesthetics, but also ethics, the sacred—and with them the possibility to live each day."[12]

Our contemporary world, seen in the context of Boehme's think-ing, is located clearly in the first triad of the sevenfold cycle.

It is not by chance that science is the dominant language of the age—as I have said, it explores precisely this first triad.

It is not by chance that for the first time in history man has acquired the means for the total, complete destruction of his own species. "Thou seest also," Boehme writes prophetically, "how the wrath of God lieth hid and resteth in the *outermost birth* of nature, and *cannot* be awakened, unless men *themselves* rouse or awaken it, who with their fleshly birth or geniture qualify, operate or unite with the wrath of the *outermost* birth of nature."[13] Indeed, man has succeeded precisely in awakening an incredible energy hidden in the deepest part of Nature, an energy capable of burning up the whole earth.

It is not by chance that for the first time in his history man is being given the means to modify the human being by changing his genetic makeup. There also we are quite close to the frontier of the magical source of reality, with all that that implies about the danger of self-destruction.

It is not by chance that this century has seen more and more monstrous wars take place, in this collective madness which represents the process of the mutual destruction of mankind. It is not by chance that we are witnessing more and more indifferently the establishment of violence in our everyday life. It is not by chance that we have seen in this century, in the name of good principles, the birth of all sorts of totalitarianism which destroy the very existence of entire peoples. To the age-old question "Why are the children of darkness more cunning than those of the light?" Jacob Boehme gives us this answer which is at once surprising and logically simple: "Why? Because they have the magical root of the original of all essences manifest in them."[14]

Our world is effectively inside the wheel of anguish, in the first triad of the sevenfold cycle. But this first triad is not *yet* closed up on itself. We are at a point of choosing the road between self-destruction and evolution. The first triad, the wheel of anguish, is only a stage of our own evolution.

B: MAN, HUMANITY, AND THE SEVENFOLD CYCLE

The idea of a possible evolution of man, beyond any physical or biological aspect, dominates all of Jacob Boehme's thought. An entire book could be written, consecrated exclusively to this idea, but here I can try to bring only a few illuminations, in relation to the subject which interests us—that of a new Philosophy of Nature.

In Boehme's perspective, evolution cannot be dissociated from the completion of the sevenfold cycle, in the orientation with which it is naturally associated—a movement from its first quality towards its last quality. In particular, this evolution cannot take place without *the discontinuous leap* between the first triad and the other four qualities of the sevenfold cycle (see Chapter Three). But, there is a fundamental difference between these two parts of the cycle, separated by the frontier of discontinuity: the qualities of the wheel of anguish are outside the will of man (they bring into play the forces which condition the passage to manifestation), while the other four require the participation of man, his will, and his consciousness. In Boehme's perspective, *man's evolution is the evolution of his consciousness.*

For Boehme, "natural man . . . moveth between two Principles"[15]; he is a "two-fold man."[16] On the one hand, the wheel of anguish is at work in him, it takes part in his constitution as a natural system. If man locks himself inside this wheel of anguish, it is like a living death, "so altogether *dead* in death, and so bolted up in the outermost birth or geniture in the dead palpability."[17] But he can evolve toward the world of light "for if the light be in him, he is born in all the three Principles; but yet he is only a spark risen from thence, and not the great source, or fountain, which is God himself."[18]

Thus it can be affirmed that the first triad of the sevenfold cycle corresponds to the body of man in all his physical and chemical aspects, and that the first discontinuity introduces him into the world of life, where the evolution of his own being can begin.

This view of a possible evolution of man is not necessarily in contradiction with the theories of evolution of modern science. After all, science recognizes that the *physical* evolution of living species leading up to man is probably accomplished, finished. We can conclude that if evolution continues, it will be able to occur only on another plane—that of culture, of consciousness, or of humanity as a collective body of all mankind.

For Boehme, conscious human evolution is a difficult process, based on self-observation, on attention, on great effort, "and man cannot better prove or try himself than by giving serious attention to what his desire and longing impel him. . . . But there must be real earnestness; for he must subdue the astral spirit which rules in him . . . For, to subdue this astral spirit, no wisdom nor art will avail; but sobriety of life, with continual withdrawal from the influxes. The elements continually introduce the astral craving into his will. Therefore it is not so easy a thing to become a child of God; it requires great labour, with much travail and suffering."[19]

This spirit of the stars pushes man endlessly toward the wheel of anguish. It has led to the creation of the visible world, of the earth, the stars, the galaxies. It is near the magical source of creation, to the devouring fire. To disengage from this astral influence signifies the reestablishment of the direction of the sevenfold cycle leading to the body of light. That is why the wonder and the fascination of the visible world, when they are taken as absolutes, are paradoxically perverse guides, for they turn back the course of the sevenfold cycle and transform evolution into involution.

The spirit of the stars leads man to believe in the complete power of the "outer body," but "the outer body has no power to move the light-world; it has only introduced itself into the world of light, whereby the light-world is become extinguished in man. He has, however, remained to be the dark world in himself; and the light-world stands in him immoveable, it is in him as it were hidden."[20]

As God dies in order to be born, man must die *in this life* in order to be born. His life thus comprises two births: biological birth and a self-birth or self-engendering. This new birth is a birth from above, for it presupposes the completion of the sevenfold cycle. The new birth implies death to oneself, a singular, mysterious process which takes place in the secrecy of the interior life. The second triad of the sevenfold cycle is a preparation for this new birth, which is brought forth only at the moment of the second discontinuity of the cycle, when "in the fountain or well-spring of the *heart* there riseth up the flash in the *sensibility* or thoughts of the brain, and therein the spirit doth contemplate or meditate."[21] Finally, the third triad of the sevenfold cycle, during the course of which "the soul eateth of God,"[22] and leads to the creation of the new body.

The responsibility of man is immense, for, in Boehme's perspective, the non-completion of his sevenfold cycle leads to a cosmic catastrophe. The entire universe of the creation would disappear in the chaos. That is why Boehme tells us, "Therefore seek for the noble Pearl; it is much more precious than this world."[23] Our smallest actions or thoughts have a cosmic dimension: "whatsoever thou buildest and sowest here in the *spirit*, be it with words, works or thoughts, *that* will be thy eternal house."[24]

It is necessary to distinguish clearly the evolution of the individual human being from the evolution of humanity. Humanity, as a collective body of all mankind, obviously submits to other laws than a man by himself. Its sevenfold cycle is different from that of one person.

The two sevenfold cycles are indeed in perpetual interaction: the one cannot develop without the other. Let us try to imagine for an instant the earth peopled in a definitive way by a single human being. The absurdity of this situation is obvious. The individual defines himself by interaction with others.

But there is an asymmetry between the two sevenfold cycles, related to the rhythm of their development. If Boehme's cosmology is true, the founders of the great religions, the great mystics, the great poets—and also an anonymous crowd whose names will never be remembered—have probably completed their sevenfold cycle in the course of their lifetime, a very short period of time compared to the age of our universe or the period corresponding to the appearance of human beings on earth. The rhythm of development of the sevenfold cycle of humanity is a great deal slower, in accord with the cosmic rhythms ruling the formation of planets, galaxies, and our universe.

Is it absurd to hypothesize a sevenfold cycle of humanity, with the underlying idea of a *unity* of humanity? Is it the product of simple speculation, with no foundation? The most rigorous approach to this question seems to me to be that furnished by contemporary research in the history of beliefs and religious ideas, of which the uncontested master is Mircea Eliade.[25] What strikes me in the first place in the work of Eliade is his discovery, based on scientific method, of a hidden driving force in the spiritual growth of humanity, through surprising convergences between different civilizations, in spite of their separation in space and time. "What seems to me totally impossible, at all events," Eliade states, "is to imagine how the human mind could function without the conviction that there is something irreducibly *real* in the world. . . . Consciousness of a real and meaningful world is intimately linked with the discovery of the sacred . . . the sacred is not a stage in the history of consciousness, it is a structural element *of* that consciousness."[26]

If we take seriously the hypothesis of a sevenfold cycle governing the evolution of humanity, this thinking layer of the earth, a first sign that the hypothesis is correct will be the appearance of a planetary civilization, where all violence of man against man, of one nation against another, will be completely abolished. Obviously we are a very long way from such a situation, even if a few facts seem to be pointing in this direction. Science is already a planetary language. The dizzying development of the computer system database establishes a communication between all points on the earth, by the creation of a sort of planetary brain. The interaction among all nations of the earth on the level of economics becomes more and more obvious. Even the menace of total destruction of our own species seems paradoxically to carry a positive message: humanity must evolve or disappear.

But where is our humanity in the development of its sevenfold cycle? All the ideas that we have outlined in this chapter lead us to the conclusion that we find ourselves in the first triad of the sevenfold cycle, inside the wheel of anguish, more precisely at the frontier of the second triad. A first discontinuity must necessarily occur to assure the passage of humanity towards *life*, if we are not going to founder in the self-destructive cycle of the wheel.

Our conclusion may indeed shock the many minds who, even if they accept the idea of an evolution of humanity (in any case a rare occurrence), are convinced that we are at a stage a good deal more evolved than that of the wheel of anguish. But, after all, humanity is very young. Its existence covers an infinitesimal period in the history of the universe. Let us imagine a book where each line covers the history of a thousand years, each page having forty lines. Thus the history of the universe would fill a library of a thousand books, each having 375 pages. The history of humanity would cover only the last 50 pages of the thousandth volume of the history of the universe. It is comprehensible that humanity finds itself at the very beginning of its evolution, just before its first step towards a self-engendering which leads to the creation of its own *body*.

The main event which seems to me to dominate this century is fundamental science's discovery by its own methods of the frontiers where it can begin a dialogue with the wisdom of the ages and with other forms of knowledge. These other forms of knowledge — art, Tradition, or the human sciences — are concerned with one or another of the four last qualities of the sevenfold cycle. But, paradoxically, it is modern science, immersed in the study of so-called "external" nature — the wheel of anguish — which today demands passage beyond the wheel in our own evolution. But this passage cannot occur on its own. A transdisciplinary dialogue between all forms of knowledge can help us bring this about — a dialogue which, without leading to a new scientism, must nonetheless take as its point of departure the contemporary discoveries of fundamental science. In this way it will find what there is *between* the different forms of knowledge, which in fact belongs to neither one form nor the other, but which ultimately circulates between the different disciplines, while respecting their autonomy. It will thus contribute to the establishment of a true, long-term, planetary dialogue, as a condition for our evolution of being.

NOTES

1. Jacob Boehme, *Mysterium Magnum*, translated by John Sparrow, 1654 (London: John M. Watkins, 1924, o.p.), VIII:24; p. 44.
2. Jacob Boehme, *The Aurora*, translated into English by John Sparrow, original edition published in 1656 (London: John M. Watkins, 1960, o.p.), II:7; p. 51.
3. *Ibid.*, I:3; p. 39.
4. *Ibid.*, XXI:110; p. 574.
5. *Mysterium Magnum*, VIII:27; p. 45.
6. Jacob Boehme, *Concerning the Three Principles of the Divine Essence*, translated by John Sparrow, 1648 (London: John M. Watkins, 1910, o.p.), XXV:70; p. 709.
7. Pierre Deghaye, *La Naissance de Dieu ou La doctrine de Jakob Boehme* (Paris: Albin Michel, Collection *Spiritualités Vivantes*, 1985), p. 156.
8. *Aurora*, IV:56; p. 98.
9. *Ibid.*, X:118-120; pp. 233-234.
10. *Ibid.*, XIX:34; p. 493.
11. *Mysterium Magnum*, III:23; p. 14.
12. Michel Henry, *La Barbarie* (Paris: Grasset, 1987), p. 9.
13. *Aurora*, XIX:130; pp. 516-517.
14. *Mysterium Magnum*, IX:16; p. 51.

15. *Three Principles*, VII:1; p. 87.

16. *Ibid.*, VII:2; p. 87.

17. *Aurora*, XXII:31; p. 590.

18. *Three Principles*, VII:2; p. 88.

19. Jacob Boehme, *Mysterium Pansophicum, or A Fundamental Statement Concerning the Earthly and Heavenly Mystery*, written in 1620. Translated by John Rolleston Earle as part of *Six Theosophic Points and Other Writings* (New York: Alfred A. Knopf, 1920, o.p.), IX:1-2; p. 172.

20. Jacob Boehme, *Sex Puncta Theosophica, or High and Deep Grounding of Six Theosophic Points: An Open Gate to All the Secrets of Life Wherein the Causes of All Being Become Known*, written in the year 1620. Translated into English by John Rolleston Earle as part of *Six Theosophic Points and Other Writings* (New York: Alfred A. Knopf, 1920, o.p.), II:39; p. 41.

21. *Aurora*, XI: 129; p. 262.

22. *Three Principles*, X:15; p. 159.

23. *Ibid.*, IX:46; p. 149.

24. *Aurora*, XVIII:49; p. 463.

25. It is necessary to read all the work of Eliade in order to realize fully the meaning of this statement. But an initial approach can be made by reading his *History of Religious Ideas*, Vol. 1: *From the Stone Age to the Eleusinian Mysteries*, translated by Willard R. Trask (Chicago: University of Chicago Press, 1979); Vol. 2: *From Gautama Buddha to the Triumph of Christianity*, translated by Willard R. Trask (Chicago: University of Chicago Press, 1984); Vol. 3: *From Muhammad to the Age of Reforms*, translated by Alf Hiltebeiten and Diane Apostolos-Cappadona (Chicago: University of Chicago Press, 1985).

26. Mircea Eliade, *Ordeal by Labyrinth: Conversations with Claude-Henri Rocquet*, translated by Derek Coltman (Chicago: University of Chicago Press, 1982), pp. 153-154.

CHAPTER SEVEN

Complexity and
Levels of Reality

N THE beginning there was complexity," Edgar
Morin writes in a dazzling formulation.[1]

In fact, our world seems invaded by "complexity." Everywhere we look, towards the infinitely
large or the infinitely small, or even at our own
scale, we see complexity manifesting itself trium-
phantly. Contemporary man moves like a stranger through an increasingly incomprehensible world, the slave of his analytical
thinking.

The dream of a "universal physics" which would explain *everything*
on the basis of a few general laws or a few fundamental building blocks
of matter has vanished with the advances of contemporary science
itself, without any interference from considerations of a philosophical
or ideological order. Even the so-called "unification" theories in particle physics, as fascinating as they might be, are concerned after all
only with physical interactions. Moreover, the unification of all
physical interactions takes place at incredible energy levels which
could never be attained in our particle accelerators.[2] Only a few more
or less out-dated scientists, for reasons more ideological than scientific, take it upon themselves to soothe public opinion with the illusion of a simplicity that is accessible by reason and science alone.

The urgency of formulating an epistemology of complexity, like
that which Edgar Morin is elaborating,[3] is an immediate reality. It is
not just a question of an attempt to introduce order into complexity so
that we can understand what is happening in natural systems: our very
life, individual and social, is directly concerned with the formulation
of a new epistemology. Is it possible to conceive of the emergence of a

new system of values and a new ethics without an understanding of this intrusive complexity, which, if it is left to proliferate according to its own chaotic and anarchic laws, can only lead to the destruction of our life and our species?

Here I would like to outline how the concept of "levels of reality" could contribute to the formulation of an epistemology of complexity.

The discovery (at the same time abstract and palpable, experimental and theoretical) of a scale "invisible" to the sense organs—*the quantum scale*, where the laws are completely different from those of the "visible" scale of our everyday life—probably has been the most important contribution that modern science has made to knowledge. The new concept which has thus emerged—that of *levels of materiality* or *levels of reality*—is one on which a new vision of the world can be based.

But is it truly a question of a new concept? I have used the expression "levels of reality" frequently throughout this book, in the symbolic sense which emerges from the cosmology of Jacob Boehme, based on the relationship between the threefold structure and the sevenfold self-organization of reality. Such a reading is too vast, too general to be applied to the results of modern science. It would be absurd, a mere caricature, to wish to bring at any price a cosmic dimension down to an earthly dimension. Moreover, the very clear difference between the methodologies of Tradition and of modern science foreshadows the failure of any hasty reconciliation between traditional and scientific thought. Finally, as Antoine Faivre remarks,[4] though true Tradition is intimately linked to the existence of a Philosophy of Nature (which is precisely the thought of Jacob Boehme and that of his followers), up until now modern science has been able to dispense with the need to formulate it. But the fact is that since the birth of quantum physics, this necessity appears more and more urgent. The formulation of this new philosophy may even, in the long run, permit a deepened dialogue between modern science and Tradition. But for the moment, we are only at the stammering stages in this dialogue, and it is urgent to advance in this direction with great prudence and by very small steps if we do not want to spoil an extraordinary potential of our age.

So let us adopt a definition of the concept of "levels of reality" which is a good deal narrower than Boehme's, but which will have the advantage of being very close to what modern science teaches us. This idea is therefore new, in a sense. It has not been brought about by a vision or by a metaphysical speculation. The concept of "levels of reality," as it will be used in the following text, is supported by scientific theory and experiment. We can say that it appears as a facet of Boehme's symbol, engendered by the dialogue between humanity and Nature over the course of time. It is a question of a *new* facet, for it is precisely the product of historical time. Boehme's symbol can only be enriched by this contribution of time; its own existence in time is what allows this enrichment.

Let me first of all give a description, although it must necessarily be an approximate one, of the meaning that I attribute to the words "reality" and "level."

I use the word "reality" in its very simple meaning, in the way the physicist experiences it in his daily work. In our practice, we continually encounter a "something" called nature, which resists our theories and our experiments. This resistance naturally gives that "something" the attribute of "reality." Likewise, the relentless resistance explains why there are never definite answers in science, but always partial, approximate ones, subject to constant change. But if there are no definitive answers, there is nonetheless a continual deepening of questioning.

The "reality" of which I am speaking is not simply a creation of the mind, to the extent that it does not allow any kind of description whatsoever; neither is it something in itself, for we intervene in an essential way and inevitably in the quantum domain with our experimental measuring process, with our mathematical formulation, with our interpretation. This reality is not a reality in itself about which anything can be said (but, it seems, a great deal can be written), nor is it an empirical reality, mute on the plane of being. It is rather a reality of interaction or participation.

Let me now define precisely the word "level."

We can describe a level (or scale) of reality as being a group of systems which remain unchanged under the action of certain transformations. For example, we can conceive of "the particle scale," "the human scale," or "the planetary scale," with humanity appearing as the interface between the systems belonging to the first level and the last.

This description is a little imprecise, for it can lead to a confusion with the ideas of levels of integration or levels of organization, such as those which appear, for example, in contemporary systemic thought.[5]

I believe that in order for a truly different level of reality to be seen, there must be a breakdown of language, a breakdown of logic, a breakdown of fundamental concepts (such as causality, for example). In this sense, the quantum level can be recognized as a level of reality different from that which corresponds to our own macroscopic scale.

I have analyzed these breakdowns at length elsewhere.[6] Here I will give just a few examples.

Our macroscopic world is characterized by the *separability* between different objects which comprise it, while in the quantum world, there appears to be an inner *non-separability*. The different interacting quantum entities, while each remaining distinct, behave simultaneously as if they formed an inseparable whole. Is quantum non-separability a particular example of a generalized non-separability of the whole universe, of the kind which is described in the work of Jacob Boehme?

Local causality, essential for classical physics, gives place to a very delicate causality, *a global causality*, which, not to be confused with ordinary finality, nevertheless determines the evolution of all the systems interacting together. Is this global causality a sign, or a particular example, of that global causality that characterizes the self-organization of Boehme's universe?

Finally, if classical thinking is based on the idea of continuity, quantum physics makes evident the crucial role of discontinuity. Where does discontinuity come from? Is it not brought about by *the interaction* between different levels of reality? Is not discontinuity manifesting itself at a certain level of reality therefore a sign of the unity of the universe, a unity precisely conditioned by its diversity?

It is very clear that, in a universe characterized by a structure of levels of reality, the passage from one level to another becomes an urgent necessity. The scope of this problem was recognized by the founding fathers of quantum mechanics, especially by Niels Bohr.

The problem of translation from one level of reality to another is intimately linked to the understanding of the nature of complexity.

We must thus distinguish *two types of complexity*: the complexity which refers to only one level of reality and the complexity which makes several levels of reality come together.

The complexity appearing at only one level of reality can be, in a way, "structured" by the idea of "level of integration"; so it is understandable why there must not be a confusion between the idea of "level of integration" and that of "level of reality." There is no one-to-one correspondence between these two ideas. In general, several "levels of integration" belong to a single "level of reality." For example, classical mechanics, organic chemistry, and classical economic thinking each set into play the same type of ideas, even if they correspond to different levels of integration.

On the other hand, the passage from one level of reality to another arouses a complexity of a completely different nature, demanding new tools of conceptual approach.

The contradictory relationship between simplicity and complexity clarifies itself in a new way: what appears to be horribly complicated at a certain level of reality can appear extremely simple at another. For example, according to the superstring theory in particle physics, physical interactions appear to be very simple and unified as a result of a few general principles, if they are depicted in a multidimensional space-time of ten dimensions (one of time and the others of space) and at an ultra-high energy, corresponding to the so-called Planck-mass. Complications arise at the moment of passage to our world, which is inevitably characterized by only four dimensions and by the fact that considerably lower energies are available.

This last remark allows me to stress the probable role of the nature of space-time in the definition of a level of reality and thus in the understanding of the nature of complexity.

Our space-time continuum of four dimensions is not the only one conceivable. In certain physical theories, it seems more like an approximation, like a "section" of a space-time a good deal richer in terms of possible phenomena. The conceptual implications of such a situation are considerable. Let us try to imagine an intelligent being, living in two-dimensional space (for example, on a sheet of paper). For him, in his own world of two dimensions, practically everything which derives from our three-dimensional world is experienced as a miracle, as an irrational, incomprehensible phenomenon.[7] It seems important to add that the supplementary dimensions appearing in theories of contemporary physics are not the result of simple intellectual speculation. On the one hand, these dimensions are necessary to assure the self-consistency of the theory and the elimination of certain undesirable aspects. On the other hand, they do not have a purely formal character—they have physical consequences on our own scale. For example, according to certain physical theories, if the universe was associated with a multidimensional space-time at the beginning of the Big Bang, then the "spontaneous compactification" of the supplementary dimensions of space (that is, their rapid rolling up into an infinitesimal region of space) can be linked to a period of very rapid exponential expansion of the universe in our usual three-dimensional space. The supplementary dimensions will remain hidden and unobservable forever, but their vestiges would be precisely the known physical interactions.

In generalizing the example furnished by particle physics, it is not absurd to think that each level of reality corresponds to a specific space-time, distinct from that of any other level of reality.

Without an appropriate translation in the passage from one level of reality to another, an endless series of paradoxes is engendered.

Thus the source of the arising of *contradiction* can be recognized; what appears as harmonious at a certain level of reality can appear paradoxical at another. That, I believe, is the source of the paradoxes engendered by the interpenetration of the terminology of quantum physics into ordinary language, paradoxes we wrongly call "quantum paradoxes": they are rather "macrophysical paradoxes," arising at the moment of translation to our own level.

In ordinary language, we are forced to describe a quantum event as either a wave or a particle. But, in its own language, that of quantum formulation, the quantum event is *simultaneously* both wave and particle, or, more precisely, it is neither wave nor particle. The quantum event is a new type of entity, which is not entirely reducible to its classical components. All the work of Stéphane Lupasco (which is based on quantum physics), and in particular his "systemology,"[8] testifies to the unsuspected richness of a logic of "contradiction."

It is interesting in this context to recall that the cosmology of Jacob Boehme, as we have mentioned several times, is founded on the dynamic of contradictory opposites. "In Nature," Jacob Boehme writes, "one thing is always opposed to another, so that one is the opposite of the other and its enemy. However, this is not to make the creatures take a mutual aversion or dislike to each other, but to keep them in motion by their struggle and their opposition, so that they can manifest themselves thus, so that great mystery can enter into their differences and their separations, and so that there can be a perfect exaltation of joy and felicity within the Eternal One."[9]

It is natural to define the different levels of reality according to our own level, in the way they are experienced by our body and our sense organs.

We are not the center of this succession of levels, but the natural system of reference.

With respect to ourselves, we can recognize the existence of levels which are nearer or farther away.

In any case, we are those who, alone among the other natural systems of the planet, seem to be equipped with a capacity for translating this information between levels.

This capacity for translation, associated with the scientific study of natural systems, allows us to pass beyond the modern illusion of a *single* level of reality, an illusion which has as its source the taking as absolute the information given by our body or our sense organs (and also, of course, the extension of these perceptions by various measuring instruments).

Our age is thus potentially that of *the abolition of the single* (one logic, one language, one causality, one space-time, one reality, one knowledge) and of *the emergence of the plural* (logics, languages, causalities, space-times, different levels of reality, different types of knowledge). There is, in this emergence of plurality, a considerable source of tolerance, which does not result from an ethical choice, but has a character of necessity in order to be in accord with the information furnished by natural systems.

The structure of levels of reality permits us to understand the resurgence of *meaning* in modern physics. In general, as Raymond Ledrut states,[10] it could be affirmed that meaning arises out of the contradictory relationship between a presence and an absence. It is the evocation of an absence in the observed reality. (I employ the word "presence" in order to signify the presence on a certain level of reality, which implies "absence" on other levels of reality. These ideas are non-static: they are evolving, for they depend on effective *translation* from one level of reality to another.)

We can thus understand why science represents moments of *the history of the real*. The role of historic time, through the action of the imaginal, is to let us embrace more and more simultaneously the richness of different levels of reality. In a certain sense, it could even be said that the imaginal becomes concrete via the different levels of reality.

The advances of modern science thus let us foresee the birth of a new rationality, infinitely richer than that bequeathed to us by the scientistic vanity of the nineteenth century.

One could even speak of the existence of different *degrees of reason* being in a one-to-one correspondence with different levels of reality. The passage from one degree of reason to another is a painful process, for it puts us into question, it demands the change of all our habits of thinking. This process corresponds to a true conversion. Of course, this conversion cannot arise from science itself; it can only be individual, for it requires a great deal more than knowledge of mathematical formulation or the data of scientific experiment.

On the social level, I believe that the decadence of our age and its evident powerlessness in facing multiple challenges are intimately linked to the blinding of science with respect to being, conjoined with the existence of a major discrepancy between the new vision of the world that is emerging from the study of natural systems and the old-fashioned values still dominating philosophy, the human sciences, and the life of modern society—values based in large measure on mechanistic determinism, positivism, or nihilism.

The opening of science toward meaning, toward being, can take place if, in particular, the idea of levels of reality is present. It permits the integration of the subject as the explorer of these levels of reality.

Scientific knowledge, by its own internal movement, has arrived at the frontiers where it must again take up an active and fruitful dialogue with other forms of knowledge. The fact that scientists themselves are beginning to wish for such a dialogue[11] seems to me very significant.

In this context, it might be asked if there are not laws of correspondences, that is to say, laws that cross several levels of reality. Their effects would be different according to the scale on which they manifest, but the laws always remain the same.

The idea of a correspondence between different planes of knowledge is not a new idea. It underlies the celebrated dialogue between Carl Gustav Jung and Wolfgang Pauli. It appears also in the works of Ludwig von Bertalanffy and Stéphane Lupasco. Niels Bohr, in fact, did not hesitate to establish correlations between sociology, politics, and physics, starting from a generalization of the complementarity principle discovered in quantum physics.

Reality could be compared to a crystal with different facets. If one facet of the crystal is removed, the crystal ceases to exist. But if there is a crystal, this signifies that there has been crystallization, that is, laws globally engendering the different facets of the crystal. It is exactly in this sense that I employ the term "correspondences." The discovery of the laws of correspondence can develop only by a new scientific and cultural approach—one which is transdisciplinary—in which all the branches of knowledge, both the so-called "exact" sciences and the so-called "human" sciences as well as art and Tradition, must cooperate.

It is important to distinguish carefully the transdisciplinary approach from others which seem to be quite similar—such as the pluridisciplinary, the multidisciplinary, or the interdisciplinary approach—but which are actually, in both their means and their ends, radically different.

The transdisciplinary approach is not concerned with the simple transfer of a model from one branch of knowledge to another, but with the study of correspondences between different fields of knowledge. In other words, it takes into account the consequences of a flow of data circulating from one branch of knowledge to another, permitting the emergence of unity in diversity and of diversity through unity. Its objective is to discover the nature and the characteristics of this flow of data and its primary task consists in elaborating a new language, a new logic, new concepts to allow the arising of a true dialogue between specialists of different branches of knowledge—a dialogue which would then open fully to the ordinary life of society and which in the long run will supply its contribution to the emergence of a true planetary dialogue.

To conclude, I will say that in confronting the problem of complexity that invades our modern world, there are three possible attitudes, attitudes which can be clearly demonstrated in the present debate about culture and about different types of knowledge.

The position of the *scientistic* type is based on the belief that a single type of knowledge—Science, Philosophy, Tradition, etc.—has the only right-of-way to truth and reality. For example, the scientistic ideology of the nineteenth century proclaimed that science alone could lead us to this goal. The happiness of humanity therefore (alas!) appeared within hand's reach. Any other means of knowledge was considered either destructive (religion, Tradition) or accessory (art). The word "science" could be replaced by the phrase "dogmatic Tradition" and science and culture could be designated as destructive ways. One could also replace "science" by "philosophy" or "culture" and consider, as did Michel Henry in his nevertheless very remarkable book, *La Barbarie*,[12] that it is precisely science which is the devil, the separator, the destroyer. In my opinion, the source of modern barbarity is not science, but the anarchic proliferation of technology and the predominance of binary logic, that of "yes" *or* "no." Modern fundamental science is a part of our culture and can contribute to the re-enchantment of the world.

A second position is that of relativism of the neo-reductionist type, formulated by Henri Atlan in his last book, *À Tort et à raison*,[13] a position which will be quick to gain a great many disciples, for it seems to be a good deal more seductive than the scientistic approach. However, the two attitudes resemble each other very much: neo-reductionist relativism is only a sort of "generalized scientism": For example, Atlan proclaims the existence of an impassable barrier and an incommensurability between mysticism and science, which nonetheless does not prevent him from trying to bring about a dialogue in his book between Talmudic tradition and modern science. Atlan comes to this conclusion starting from the postulate that each of these two approaches "takes the position from the outset that its [own] relevance is unlimited and that it is capable, in principle, of accounting for everything that exists."[14] As a result, he denies the value of all search for a meta-discourse or a meta-theory. Everything thus becomes fun and games: one can amuse oneself hopping from one branch of knowledge to another, but cannot find any bridge linking them.

Here is an important difference from the relativism of the transdisciplinary type which I advocate: While recognizing the autonomy of each field of knowledge and the essential differences between various ways of knowing, transdisciplinary relativism is based on the idea that none of these ways could embrace reality as a whole. The search for correspondences is not to be confused with the search for the one and only logic of logics, to the extent that we must always formulate models which are successive approximations. Historic time and approximation will always go together. Transdisciplinary relativism, rigorously conducted, could never end in a globalized discourse, in a closed system of thought, in a new utopia. It refuses all bondage to one ideology, one religion, or one system of philosophy—whatever they may be.

Totality is a phantasm, and separateness is also a phantasm. I believe that it is good to avoid both. But certainly it is very difficult for us to conceive of the unity of contradictory opposites.

An interesting example is the recent birth of a new truly transdisciplinary branch of science—*quantum cosmology*. As its name indicates, this new science is based on the idea of the unity between two scales of nature which were considered, until just a few years ago, as completely different—the quantum scale and the cosmological scale. The interactions between particles can teach us about the evolution of the cosmos, and data about cosmological dynamics can clarify certain aspects of particle physics. Quantum cosmology revolves around the idea of the spontaneous appearance of the universe, as the result of laws of physics. The universe seems capable of creating itself and also of organizing itself, with no "outside" intervention. The most appropriate image for visualizing this self-contained dynamic of the uni-

verse would be the ouroboros—the serpent which bites its own tail—
an ancient gnostic symbol and also the symbol of the completion of the
Great Work in alchemy.

This example foreshadows the richness of a transdisciplinary kind
of research. A true dynamic of the bootstrap type (self-consistency)
could be envisaged between different levels of reality: *each level of
reality is what it is because all other levels of reality exist at the same time.* A
meta-discourse or a meta-theory would therefore be possible, but they
would never be unique or absolute.

While located resolutely in the domain of the rational, the transdisciplinary approach would permit the emergence of a polyphonic
dialogue, between rational and irrational, sacred and profane, simplicity and complexity, unity and diversity, nature and the imaginal,
man and the universe. I am convinced that in the decades to come it
could establish itself as the preferred means for developing the epistemology of complexity and could light the way to the formulation of a
new Philosophy of Nature.

NOTES

1. Edgar Morin, *La Méthode*, vol. 1: *La Nature de la nature* (Paris: Seuil, 1977), p. 149.
2. Physicists currently speak of a "Theory of Everything," already referred to by the initials
   TOE. But we must not mistake words for realities: it is a question of only one of those
   sensational terminological findings which physicists are so eager for. All serious physicists
   know the limitations of this theory, which is moreover still not fully formulated: it is only
   in a state of gestation.
3. See also (in addition to the above-cited work) Edgar Morin, *La Méthode*, vol. II: *La Vie de
   la vie* (Paris: Seuil, 1980), and vol. III: *La Connaissance de la connaissance—1. Anthro-
   pologie de la connaissance* (Paris: Seuil, 1986).
4. Antoine Faivre, *Accès de l'ésotérisme occidental* (Paris: Gallimard, Bibliothèque des Sciences Humaines, 1986).
5. See, for example, Ervin Laszlo, *Le Systémisme—vision nouvelle du monde* (Paris: Pergamon
   Press, 1981)[*The Systems View of the World* (New York: George Braziller, Inc., 1972]; and
   Erich Jantsch, *The Self-Organizing Universe* (Elmsford, NY: Pergamon, 1980).
6. Basarab Nicolescu, *Nous, la particule et le monde* (Paris: Le Mail, 1985).
7. For a good popularization of multidimensional space (hyperspace), see Rudy Rucker, *The
   Fourth Dimension* (Boston: Houghton Mifflin Company, 1984).
8. Stéphane Lupasco, *L'Expérience microphysique et la pensée humaine* (Paris: P.U.F., 1941);
   Le principe d'antagonisme et la logique de l'énergie (Paris: Le Rocher, 1987), Collection
   l'Ésprit et la Matière, preface by Basarab Nicolescu; *Qu'est-ce qu'une structure?* (Paris:
   Christian Bourgois, 1967); *Les Trois Matières* (Strasbourg: Éditions Cohérence, 1982).
9. Jacob Boehme, *De l'élection de la grâce*, French translation by Debeo (Milan: Arché,
   1976), pp. 27-28.

10. Raymond Ledrut, *Situation de l'Imaginaire dans la dialectique du rationnel et de l'irrationnel*, in *Cahiers de l'imaginaire*, # 1, "L'Imaginaire dans les sciences et les arts," (Toulouse: Editions Privat, 1988), pp. 43-50.

11. *Science and the Boundaries of Knowledge: The Prologue of Our Cultural Past*, final report of the Colloquium of Venice, organized by UNESCO in collaboration with the Cini Foundation, Venice, March 3-7, 1986 (Paris: UNESCO, 1987); *La Science face aux confins de la connaissance—La Déclaration de Venise* (Paris: Éditions de Félin, 1987).

12. Michel Henry, *La Barbarie* (Paris: Grasset, 1987).

13. Henri Atlan, *À Tort et à raison* (Paris: Seuil, 1986).

14. *Ibid.*, p. 321.

By Way of Conclusion

AVING arrived at the end of this brief study, I am perfectly aware that I have unveiled only a very small corner of an immense territory. But I had to bear witness to my encounter with the thought of Jacob Boehme; to bear witness to my conviction that his work can make a fundamental contribution to the contemporary search for a new Philosophy of Nature; to bear witness to a possible reenchantment of the world through the encounter between the study of man and the study of the universe.

After having explored the infinitely small and the infinitely large, man finds himself confronted with the endless complexity of the encounter with himself.

The ambiguity of our age is fascinating. Everything seems to be arranged for our confinement in the "wheel of anguish," for our self-destruction, our disappearance as a species from the surface of this earth. But at the same time, everything seems to be in position for the emergence of a new Renaissance, of a scope incommensurable with that of the movement which spanned the sixteenth and the seventeenth centuries. It is about the possibility of this New Renaissance that I have wished to bear witness.

But what are the tangible marks of the potential for such a new Renaissance, if we want to pass beyond pure verbiage or the declarations of intent with no real substance?

First of all, there is the quest for the identity of Europe. We speak a great deal, and rightly so, of the importance of the build-up of Europe in this dawning of the twenty-first century. But, in my opinion, we will never succeed in realizing this build-up if we limit ourselves to political, economical, or social motivations, however well justified. It is by the rediscovery of a spiritual bond between the different European nations that we will succeed in revealing our own identity. To respond to a question which has recurred often in this book—"Why was modern science born in the West?"—is to contribute in a direct way to this quest for the identity of Europe.

My conclusion, based on the study of Jacob Boehme's work as an exemplary case, is that the Christian contemplation of the Trinity has been the seedbed out of which modern science has sprouted. This conclusion may be surprising even if it does nothing more than extend and define other avenues of research, in particular that of Charles Morazé. The established churches have indeed scorned Nature for a long time and have cast it into an outer darkness. But Christian thought passes far beyond any institutional framework; so it is not surprising that its quintessence is often found in the work of thinkers on the fringes of the established churches, like Boehme, who was considered a "heretic" in his time. Nor is it surprising that modern science has had to define itself by a break with traditional thought, which was locked into an institutional framework that was stifling and withering it. But this break is of a methodological order: it does not in any way make a total breach with the living thought which has permitted the birth of modern science. This break in methodology has been the condition *sine qua non* for the full and spectacular development of the New Science, a development which has led to the science of our own century.

Certainly, the threefold structure of reality is found in a great many traditions. But the specific and single quality of Christian thinking on the Trinity can be strictly demonstrated. The paradoxical coexistence of the one in three and the three in one already implies the potential of manifestation of divinity through Nature. In order to come to the actualization of this potential, there was a necessity for this unique encounter between creative imagination, Christian thought, and Jacob Boehme's genius. Boehme could thus discover, in his own interior being, a true universal dynamic through the interaction between the threefold structure and the sevenfold self-organization of reality conforming to it. Christian meditation on the Trinity thus reveals all these potentials, in a prophetic explosion embracing all the cosmoses.

Nature finds its own place in this dazzling dynamic—that of the receptacle of the birth of God.

A second mark of the New Renaissance, which is moreover linked fundamentally to the one described before, is the contemporary encounter between science and meaning, a major event which will probably produce the only true revolution of this century. Contemporary science is certainly international, but its deep roots always remain anchored in the soil of its birth. More and more, science discovers its own limits, determined by its own methodology, and has more and more need of meaning, as a tree needs the air and the soil for its full development. Science has been able to examine the indications found in Nature in a magnificent way, but, because of its own methodology, it is incapable of discovering the meaning of these signs: Science, doubled back on itself and cut off from philosophy, can only lead to self-destruction because of its dominant position in our society. The self-destruction is necessarily brought about by lack of ontological understanding of these signs of Nature which are more and more numerous, more and more powerful, and more and more active. At the other pole, philosophy, wisdom, and Tradition, doubled back on themselves, through mistrust or ignorance of these signs of Nature, can only, as powerless witnesses, await their own withering and their own death. The dialogue between science and meaning becomes more necessary than ever. But how can we instigate this dialogue?

It is here that the third mark of the New Renaissance comes in. We must invent a mediation between science and meaning. This mediation can only be a new Philosophy of Nature. It would be presumptuous and on the verge of the ridiculous to try to formulate that at once. The ancient Philosophy of Nature has required several centuries to come to its full formulation; in its turn, the new Philosophy of Nature can only be formulated over a long period of patient research. We can nevertheless decipher immediately some of these incontrovertible characteristics.

A return to a cut-and-dried theology, tradition, or ideology is inconceivable. The point of departure for a new Philosophy of Nature can only be modern science, but a science which, having reached its own limits, tolerates and even demands an opening to being. This opening can take place only by a new type of scientific and cultural approach—a transdisciplinary one. This opens an incredible space for a free dialogue between the past and the present, between science, art, Tradition, and all other forms of knowledge. Through its own methods, science has discovered the existence of levels of reality. We were in "danger of death" under the domination of thinkers who extolled a single horizontal level of reality, where everything turns in circles and inevitably brings forth chaos, anarchy, and self-destruction. We are now passing into an era of "danger of life," through the recognition of different levels of reality opening a vertical, multiple, polyphonic dimension of being. The transdisciplinary approach, intimately linked with levels of reality, is the preferred means for exploring what circulates between these different levels. On this path, it is inevitable that the great texts of the past, such as those of Jacob Boehme, will be rediscovered, for culture forms an indissociable, inseparable whole, over all times. Boehme shows us how the multiple splendor of Being is reflected in the mirror of Nature; in its turn, modern science has brought about our discovery of increasingly dazzling signs while looking into this mirror. Unlike Ilya Prigogine, I am convinced that modern science's opening to being will not lead us to a return to pantheism. The recognition of an irreducible reality, the very basis of the sacred, but which manifests itself through multiple facets and which participates in our life, will open a horizon infinitely richer than that of pantheism. What we call the "real" is the result of the interaction between two facets of one and the same Reality: the physical universe and humanity. The time for a truly new alliance—that of man with himself—has come. In our quest, Jacob Boehme is present among us, bodily present, a friend, a divine cobbler, a living witness to this new alliance.

The TREE *of the* SOUL.

LIGHT OF MAJESTY

PARADISE

SOLAR
WORLD

Afterword

HE relationship between Nature and Spirit is perhaps the most fundamental question of metaphysics. Certainly it can be avoided, by asserting that only one order of reality exists: either Nature alone, reduced to matter or to a form of energy; or else (following the example of the so-called "Traditionalists") Spirit alone, outside of which everything, including Nature in its entirety, is nothing but illusion. Pantheism, which allows God no place outside of Nature, would then be a variation of this two-faced monism. One can also set a gulf between Spirit and Nature, a radical dissolution of their continuity. From this come the various styles of dualism: both that of Deism, with its tranquil *deus otiosus* (lazy god), and the tragic examples developed with a vengeance by the Gnostic schools of the Manichean type, ready to pronounce upon Nature a hopeless anathema.

On the other hand, it is possible to conceive of this relationship of Nature and Spirit as a richly paradoxical complexity. This in no way prevents one of the two terms from becoming absorbed by the other, as the result of a "dialectical" process: for example, Nature might be absorbed into a Spirit in quest of self-realization. But we are not obliged to give in to this temptation of conceiving Being, even absolute Being, as devouring its progeny! A particularly fruitful path now opens up: the path always taken in the West when an interest in Nature as a reality, not an illusion—in Nature as subject—is accompanied by the consideration of what may be, as it were, outside Nature, *i.e.*, outside what can be grasped by scientific observation and experiment. The Judeo-Christian tradition certainly carries no seed of contempt for these possiblities. Nevertheless, the recurrent temptation to repress Nature, to reduce and humiliate it, is one of the most interesting (and most disconcerting) aspects of Judeo-Christian history—this Nature which is feminine, and by that token is the Sophia praised by Jacob Boehme. The temptation is most obvious in the established churches; but even there the Middle Ages witnessed, for example, the Schools of Chartres and of Oxford, among other currents too readily forgotten. It is more often on the fringes of the churches that one finds the most inspired people: they may be attached to a church, but their relative independence or secular status allows them a certain margin of liberty. Such a person "unites God, man and the cosmos," so as to be a living "natural table of correspondences," to echo the title of Louis Claude de Saint-Martin's wonderful book [Le Tableau Naturel].

Jacob Boehme is one of these. Perhaps this master of Saint-Martin, Franz von Baader, and many others, is the greatest of them all. His writings are those of a visionary, perpetually open to the mythic realm of Judeo-Christianity. His inspiration makes it gush forth in torrential storms and showers, volcanic lava, and bouquets for the senses in tender colors, variegated and ordered like those of a rainbow. Dare one consent, purely as a hypothesis, to acknowledge in his discourse a prophetic dimension comparable to that of Ezekiel? Dare one risk agreeing that Boehme's creative imagination might not be reducible to the caprices of a self-contained subjectivity? This would not necessarily constitute an act of faith, but might be the result of a methodological wager, whose stake would certainly be worth the risk taken. It is this wager that Basarab Nicolescu invites us to make; and I think it can be accepted, for at least three reasons.

If anyone still has doubts as to whether the imagination—now taken in the very broadest sense of the term—works to direct the choice of one's studies and even influences the nature of one's discoveries, perhaps he has not yet pondered sufficiently on the potential value of structures intended to be universal, as found among certain visionaries. Each of these structures, claimed or implied by its author to be "absolute," might seem to relegate its predecessors to the status of out-of-date curiosities. But each of them would doubtless be worth using, at some time or other, by the seeker who has agreed to enter on that quest for unifying schemata; acting as an *organon* or tool, it could help him cast his nets into the waters of its representation of the Real.

Raymond Lull, Hoëné Wronski, Raymond Abellio, and Jacob Boehme are among the Western thinkers who have built such edifices. But Boehme was certainly the only one who forged his key in the visionary furnace of the mythic. He used a symbolism whose baroque design, far from hurting the internal coherence of his discourse, gives it substance and incarnates it in figurative and concrete structures.

Perhaps one has nothing to lose in postulating a commonality of nature between the human mind and the universe, so as to proceed with the hypothetical and deductive steps whose implications Basarab Nicolescu explores. This commonality means that the two terms, Mind and Universe, would be associated in an analogical relationship, such that the human mind might sometimes be capable of interiorizing, then of refracting in the form of images and symbols, the very structures which "maintain the universe in its inmost parts" ("*Was die Welt im Innersten zusammenhält*"—Goethe's *Faust*). The Alexandrian *Corpus Hermeticum* of the third century developed this notion of interiorization. And thus Raymond Abellio, struck by the close analogy revealed by a comparison of the sixty-four hexagrams of the *I Ching* with the elements of the genetic code, was able to draw attention to the possibility of such a commonality of nature.

It therefore seems to me—and this is the second reason for accepting the wager proposed by Basarab Nicolescu—that among the visionaries whose imagination presents itself directly as "creative," *i.e.*, as capable of recreating and, in a sense, of reproducing the archetypal configurations, the ones who go furthest are those who take the mythic as their basis. It becomes their foundation, the support of their meditations, their springboard and heuristic tool, endowing their work with an aura of authenticity. The mythic, here, is a story experienced in images, a scenario organized as a triptych: first cosmology (even theogony) and anthropogony; then cosmology (or cosmosophy); and lastly eschatology. The hermeneutics of this history, in Jacob Boehme, always develop on the basis of Revelation—that of Judeo-Christianity—and bear the name of Theosophy, which applies equally well to the Jewish Kabbalah of the *Zohar*.

What can it offer to us? Nothing less than the possibility of reconstituting our own caduceus. If the mythic, thus understood, were again taken seriously, thanks to those few who can escape the grasp of reductionism, it would raise the question then and there of the meaning of science and its goals, ever since the time when man has no longer felt fully at home in a nature which has tended to become radically "other." This is why one feels that urgent need for a Philosophy of Nature, in the sense understood by the German Romantic thinkers such as Franz von Baader—the "*Boehmius redivivus*" ("Boehme resurrected"). This would be a *Naturphilosophie* unrestricted by theology, and still less by ideology, but open to ontological questions and reaping the advantages of transdisciplinary study. A creative imagination like that of Jacob Boehme, plunging its roots into the soil of the mythic, just as the tree laden with flowers or fruits draws its fecundity from the earth, would thus join company, in a double bond like that of Hermes' serpent-wound staff, with a science whose specificity would no longer bar the scientist from also being a philosopher.

There is a third and final reason, linked to the first two, which concerns the very choice of Jacob Boehme by the author of the present book. Up to now, in the twentieth century, the embryonic shoots of a Philosophy of Nature which still lacks embodiment are mainly presented in the form of comparisons or resemblances between a "reality" described by science, and images borrowed from the symbolism of various religious traditions. None of this is contrary to the directions suggested above, but all the same, these resemblances, such as that between Taoism and physics, however attractive they may be, remain essentially aesthetic. For want of an ontological foundation, they cannot serve by themselves as the gateway to a Philosophy of Nature. If it is true, as Basarab Nicolescu insists, that the degrees of reality "correspond" to those of the imaginal world, the comparisons repeatedly offered us invite us to consider only the first degrees to be traversed. Finally, one notices that the vast majority of these comparisons draw on images and traditions from the Far East, as if our Western soil, still so little explored in this regard, were not ready to reveal its beauty; as if it did not contain theosophic, alchemical, and hermetic strata to be exploited, with riches doubtless more accessible than those exotic Eastern pearls. It is these strata that should orient our quest. And for this reason, too, we welcome the appearance of Basarab Nicolescu's book as an event.

—*Antoine Faivre*

Key Texts
from the Works of
Jacob Boehme

Selected by
BASARAB NICOLESCU

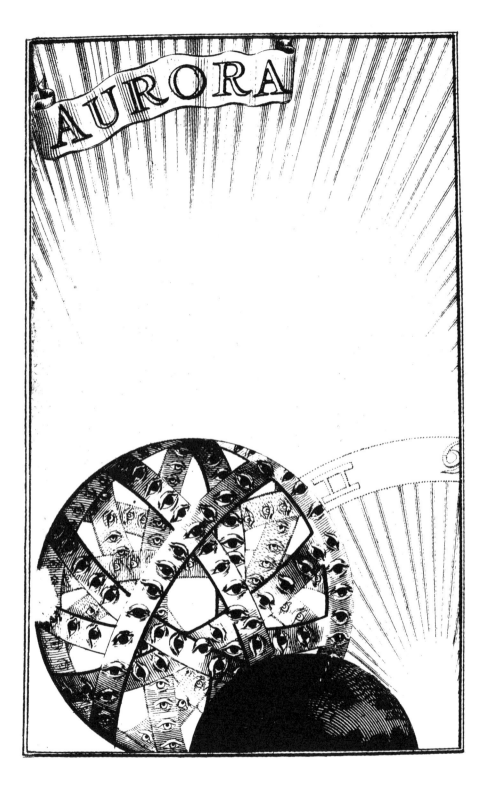

The Aurora

TRANSLATED BY JOHN SPARROW

Preface

7. The garden of this tree signifieth the *world*; the soil or mould signifieth *nature*; the stock of the tree signifies the *stars*; by the *branches* are meant the *elements*; the fruit which grow on this tree signify *men*; the sap in the tree denoteth the pure *Deity*. Now men were made out of nature, the *stars*, and *elements*; but God the Creator reigneth in all: even as the *sap* doth in the whole tree.

8. But there are two *qualities in nature*, even until the *Judgment* of God: The one is pleasant, heavenly and holy; the other is fierce, wrathful, hellish and thirsty.

9. Now the good one qualifieth and worketh continually with all industry to bring forth *good* fruit, and the *Holy Ghost* reigneth therein, and affords thereunto sap and life: the bad one springeth and driveth with all its endeavor to bring forth *bad* fruit continually, to which the devil affordeth sap and *hellish* flame. Now both are in the tree of nature, and *men* are made out of *that* tree, and live in this world, in this garden, *between* both, in great danger; suddenly the sun shineth on them; by and by, winds, rain, and snow fall on them.

16. But now man is poisoned through sin, that the fierce wrathful quality, as well as the good, reigneth in him, and he is now *half* dead, and in his gross ignorance can no more know God his Creator, nor nature and its operation: Yet hath nature used its best endeavours from the beginning till now, to which God hath given his Holy Ghost, so that it [nature] hath at all times generated wise, holy, and *understanding* men, who learned to know nature, and their Creator, and who always in their writings and teachings have been a *light* to the world, whereby God hath raised his Church on earth, to his eternal praise. Against which the devil hath *raged*, and spoiled many a noble twig, through the wrathful fierceness in nature, whose *prince* and god he is.

21. Also it is clearly seen by the *first* world, as also by the *second*, even unto the end of our time, how the heavenly and the hellish kingdoms in nature have always wrestled the one with the other, and stood in great travail, even as a woman in the birth.

26. But when the tree of nature came to its middle age, then it began to bear some *mild* and sweet fruit, to shew that it would henceforth bear pleasant fruit. Then were born the *holy prophets*, out of the sweet branch of the tree, who taught and preached of the *light*, which hereafter should overcome the wrathful fierceness in nature. And then there arose a light in nature among the Heathen, so that they knew nature, and her operation, although this was a light in the *wild* nature *only*, and was not yet the *holy* light.

27. For the wild nature was not yet overcome, and light and darkness wrestled so long the one with the other, till the *sun* arose, and with its heat forced this tree, so that it did bear pleasant sweet fruit; that is, till there came the Prince of Light, out of the heart of God, and *became man* in nature, and wrestled in his human body, in the power of the divine light, in the wild nature. That same Prince and *Royal* Twig grew up in nature, and became a tree in nature, and spread its branches abroad from the east to the west; and encompassed the whole nature, and wrestled and fought with the fierce wrath which was in nature, and with the prince thereof, till he overcame and triumphed, as a king in nature, and took the *prince of wrath* or fierceness *captive* in his own house [Psalms 68].

The Contents Of This Book

6. The supreme title is AURORA, that is, *The Dawning of the Day in the East,* or *Morning Redness in the rising of the* SUN.

It is a secret Mystery, concealed from the wise and prudent of this world, of which they themselves shall shortly be sensible: But to those who read this book in singleness of heart, with a desire after the Holy Spirit, who place their hope in God only, it will *not* be a hidden secret, but a manifest knowledge.

7. I will not explain this title, but commit it to the judgment of the *impartial* Reader, who wrestleth in the good quality of this world.

8. Now if Mr Critic, who qualifieth or worketh with his wit in the fierce quality, gets this book into his hand, he will oppose it, as there is always a stirring and opposition between the kingdom of heaven and the kingdom of hell.

I. First, he will say that I ascend too *high* into the Deity, which is not a meet thing for me to do.

II. Then, secondly, he will say that I boast of the Holy Spirit, and that I had more need to live accordingly, and make demonstration of it by wondrous works or miracles.

III. Thirdly, he will say that I am not learned *enough.*

IV. Fourthly, he will say that I do it in a vainglorious way.

V. Fifthly, he will be much offended at the *simplicity* of the author; for in the world it is usual [or customary] to be mindful only of high things, and to be irritated by simplicity.

15. So neither can I say anything of myself, nor boast or write of anything, save this: that I am a *simple* man, and, besides, a *poor sinner,* and have need to pray daily, *Lord, forgive us our sins*; and to say with the Apostle, *O Lord, thou hast redeemed us with thy blood.*

16. Neither did I ascend into heaven, and behold all the works and creatures of God; but the same heaven is *revealed* in my spirit, so that in the spirit I know the works and creatures of God.

17. Besides, the will to that is not my natural will, but it is the *impulse* of the spirit; and for it I have endured many an assault of the devil.

33. Time past, present, and to come, as also depth and height, near and afar off, are all *one* in God, one comprehensibility.

34. The holy soul of man seeth the same also, but in this world in part only. It happeneth *sometimes* that it seeth nothing at all, for the devil doth assault it furiously in the fierce wrathful source that is in the soul, and oftentimes covereth the noble mustard-seed; therefore man must always be at strife [or in conflict].

The First Chapter

OF SEARCHING OUT THE DIVINE BEING IN NATURE: OF BOTH THE QUALITIES, THE GOOD AND THE EVIL.

1. Though flesh and blood cannot conceive or apprehend the being of God, but the spirit only when enlightened and kindled from God:

2. Yet if a man will speak of God, and say what God is, then,

I. A man must diligently consider the *powers* in nature.

II. Also the whole creation, heaven and earth.

III. The stars, the elements, and the creatures that are proceeded from them. As also the holy angels, devils, and men; moreover, heaven and hell.

Of the Two Qualities in One.

3. In this consideration are found *two qualities*, a *good* one and an *evil* one, which are in each other as one thing in this world, in all powers, in the stars and the elements, as also in all the creatures; and no creature in the flesh, in the natural life, can subsist, unless it hath the two qualities.

What a Quality is.

4. Now here a man must consider what the word quality meaneth or is. A quality is the mobility, boiling, springing and driving of a thing.

Of Heat.

5. As for example, *heat*, which burneth, *consumeth* and driveth forth all whatsoever that cometh into it which is not of the same property; and again, it *enlighteneth* and warmeth all cold, wet and dark things; it compacteth and hardeneth soft things.

Of Light and Fierceness.

6. Heat containeth likewise two other kinds in it, namely, (1) Light, and (2) Fierceness; of which take notice in this manner. The light, or the heart of the heat, is in itself a pleasant, joyful glance or lustre, a power of *life*, an enlightening and glance of a thing which is afar off, which light is a piece or source of the heavenly kingdom of joy.

7. For it maketh *living* and moving all things in this world. All flesh, trees, leaves and grass grow in this world in the power of the light, and have their life therein, *viz.* in the good.

8. Again, heat containeth also a fierceness or *wrath*, which burneth, consumeth and spoileth; this wrath or fierceness springeth, driveth and elevateth itself in the light, and maketh the light moveable.

9. Heat wrestleth and fighteth together in its twofold source as one thing: It is also one thing, but it hath a double source.

The Second Chapter

AN INTRODUCTION, SHEWING HOW MEN MAY COME TO APPREHEND THE DIVINE, AND THE NATURAL, BEING. AND FURTHER OF THE TWO QUALITIES.

1. All whatsoever that hath been mentioned above is called *quality*, because it qualifieth, operateth or frameth all in the deep above the earth, also upon the earth and in the earth, in one another, as ONE thing, and yet hath several distinct virtues and operations, and but one mother, from whence descend and spring all things.

2. All the creatures are made and descended from *these qualities*, and live therein as in their mother; and the earth and stones descend or proceed from thence also; and all that groweth out of the earth liveth and springeth forth out of the virtue of these qualities; no *rational man* can deny it.

3. Now this twofold source, good and evil, in everything, is caused by the stars; for as the creatures in the earth are, in their qualities, so also are the stars.

4. For from its twofold source, everything hath its great mobility, running, springing, driving and growing. For meekness in nature is a still *rest*, but the fierceness in every power maketh all things moveable, running and generative.

5. For the driving qualities cause a lust in all creatures unto evil and good, so that all [things] are *desirous* one of another, to copulate and increase, decrease, grow fair, perish, love and hate.

Of the Quality of the Sun.

15. If thou wilt be a philosopher and *naturalist*, and search into *God's being in nature*, and discern how all is come to pass, then pray to God for the Holy Spirit, to enlighten thee with it.

16. For in thy flesh and blood thou art not able to apprehend it, and though thou dost read it, yet it is but as a fume or mist before thine eyes.

17. In the Holy Ghost alone, who is in God, and also in the whole nature, out of which all things were made, in him alone canst thou search into the whole body or corporeity of God, which is *nature*; as also into the Holy Trinity itself.

18. For the Holy Ghost goeth forth from the Holy Trinity, and reigneth and ruleth in the *whole body* or *corpus* of God; that is, in the whole nature.

19. Even as the spirit of man ruleth and reigneth in the whole body, in all the veins, and replenisheth the *whole man*; even so the Holy Ghost replenisheth the whole nature, and is the *heart* of nature, and reigneth in the good qualities of everything.

20. Now, if thou hast that spirit in thee, so that it enlighteneth, *filleth* and replenisheth thy spirit, then thou wilt understand what followeth in this writing.

21. But if not, then it will be with thee as it was with the *wise* Heathen, who gazed and stared on the creation, and would search and sift it out by their *own reason*; and though with their fictions and conceits they came before God's countenance or face, yet they were not able to see it, but were stark *blind* in the knowledge of God.

22. As the Children of *Israel* in the desert could not behold the countenance of *Moses*, and therefore, when he drew near to the people, he must put a veil before his face.

23. The cause of this was, that they neither understood nor knew the true God and his will, who, *notwithstanding*, walked among them; and therefore that veil was a sign and type of their blindness and misunderstanding.

24. As little as a piece of work can apprehend him that made it, so little also can *man* apprehend and know God his Creator, unless the Holy Ghost *enlighten* him; which happeneth only to those that rely not upon themselves, but set their *hope*, will and desires upon God alone, and move in the Holy Ghost, and these are *one spirit* with God.

25. Now if we consider rightly of the sun and stars, with their *corpus* or body, operations and qualities, then the very divine being may be found therein, and we may find that the virtues of the stars are nature itself.

28. But here thou must elevate thy mind in the *spirit,* and consider how the *whole nature*, with all the powers which are in nature, also the wideness, depth and height, also heaven and earth, and all whatsoever is therein, and all that is above the heavens, is together the *body* or corporeity of God; and the powers of the stars are the fountain veins in the natural body of God *in this world*.

29. Thou must not conceive that in the body of the stars is the *triumphing* Holy Trinity, God the Father, Son, and Holy Ghost, in which there is no evil, for it is the light-holy, eternal fountain of joy, which is indivisible and unchangeable, which no creature can sufficiently apprehend or express; which dwelleth and is above the body of the stars in itself, whose depth no creature is able to measure or fathom.

30. But we must not so conceive as if God were not at all in the *corpus* or body of the stars, and in this world: For when we say, *ALL,* or *from eternity to eternity,* or *All in All,* then we understand the entire GOD.

31. For a similitude or example take man, *who is made after the image or similitude of God,* as it is written [Genesis I:27].

79. This indeed hath been partly concealed from the beginning of the world to this time, and man with his *reason* could not comprehend it.

80. But seeing God is pleased to reveal himself in simplicity in this last time, I shall give way to his impulse and will; I am but a very little spark of light. *AMEN.*

The Third Chapter

OF THE MOST BLESSED TRIUMPHING, HOLY, HOLY, HOLY TRINITY, GOD THE FATHER, SON, AND HOLY GHOST, ONE ONLY GOD.

13. When we consider the whole nature and its property, then we see the Father.

14. When we behold heaven and the stars, then we behold his eternal *power* and wisdom: So many stars stand in the whole heaven that they are innumerable and incomprehensible to *reason,* and some of them are not visible, so manifold and [so] *various* is the power and wisdom of God the Father.

Observe here the great Mystery of God.

53. Further, the sun is made or generated from all the stars, and is a light taken from the whole nature, and shineth again into the whole nature of this world; it is *united* with the other stars, as if itself together with all the stars were but *one* star.

Of the Holy TRINITY

80. Now when we speak or write of the *three Persons* in the Deity, you must *not conceive* that therefore there are three Gods, each reigning and ruling by himself, like temporal kings on the earth.

81. No: such a substance and being is not in God; for the divine being consisteth in power, and not in body or flesh.

82. The Father is the whole divine power, whence *all creatures* have proceeded, and hath been always, from eternity: He hath neither beginning nor end.

83. The Son is in the Father, being the Father's Heart or light, and the Father generateth the Son continually, from eternity to eternity; and the Son's *power* and splendour shine back again in the whole Father, as the sun doth in the *whole* world.

84. The Son is also *another* Person than the Father, but not externally, without or severed from the Father, *nor* is he any other God than the Father is; his power, splendour, and omnipotence, are *no less* than the whole Father.

85. The Holy Ghost *proceedeth* from the Father and the Son, and is the *third* self-subsisting Person in the Deity. As the *elements* in this world go forth from the sun and the stars, and are the moving spirit which is in everything in this world,

86. So the Holy Ghost is the moving spirit in the whole Father, and proceedeth or goeth forth from eternity to eternity *continually* from the Father and the Son, and replenisheth the whole Father; he is nothing less or greater than the Father and the Son; his *moving power* is in the whole Father.

109. *Thus* you find in everything a similitude of the *Ternary* in the divine being, look upon what you will; let no man make himself so

stark blind as to think *otherwise*, or to think that God hath no Son and no Holy Ghost.

110. I shall make this *more* plain and clear when I come to write of the *creation*; for I do *not borrow* of other men in my writings: And though indeed I quote many examples and testimonies of God's saints, yet all is written by God in my mind, so that I *absolutely* and infallibly believe, know and see it; yet not in the flesh, but in the spirit, in the impulse and motion of God.

111. It is not so to be understood that my reason is greater or higher than that of all other men living; but I am the Lord's *twig* or branch, and am a very mean and little spark of his; he may set me where he pleaseth, I cannot hinder him in that.

112. Nor is this my *natural will*, that I could do it by my own small ability; for if the spirit were withdrawn from me, then I could neither know nor understand *my own writings*; and I must on every side fight and struggle with the devil, and lie open to temptation and affliction as well as other men.

113. But in the following chapters you will *soon see* the devil and his kingdom *laid naked*; his pride and reproach shall suddenly *be discovered*.

The Fifth Chapter

OF THE CORPOREAL SUBSTANCE,
BEING AND PROPRIETY OF AN ANGEL.

29. Here I write not without knowledge; but if thou, like an *epicure* and fatted swine of the devil, from the devil's instigation, shouldst *mock* at these things and say:

30. The fool surely hath *not* gone up to heaven and seen or heard them, *these* are mere fables; then, in the power of my knowledge, I would have you warned, and *cited* before the severe judgment of God.

Question.

35. The question now is, What manner of *qualification* hath an angel?

Answer.

36. The *holy soul* of a man, and the spirit of an angel, are and have one and the same substance and being, and there is no difference therein, but only in the *quality* itself, or in their corporeal government; that which qualifieth *outwardly*, or from without, in man by the air hath a *corrupt earthly* quality, yet on the other side, hidden from the creatures, it hath also a *divine* and *heavenly* quality.

37. But the *holy* soul understandeth it well, as the kingly prophet *David* saith, *The Lord rideth on the wings of the wind* [Psalms 104:3]. In the angel the divine property qualifies only in perfect holiness, divinity and purity.

Question.

38. But a simple man may ask, What do you mean by the word *qualifying*, or what is that?

Answer.

39. I mean thereby the power, which in the body of the angel *entereth in* from without, and cometh forth again; as in a similitude, when a man fetcheth breath and breatheth it forth again; for *therein* standeth the life both of the body and of the spirit.

The Seventh Chapter

OF THE COURT, PLACE AND DWELLING, ALSO THE GOVERNMENT
OF ANGELS, HOW THESE THINGS STOOD AT THE BEGINNING,
AFTER THE CREATION, AND HOW THEY BECAME AS THEY ARE.

Observe:

40. The Father's power is all, in and above all heavens, and the same power everywhere generateth the light. Now this UNIVERSAL POWER is, and is called, the *universal power* of the Father; and the light which is generated out of that universal power is, and is called, the Son.

41. But it is therefore called the Son, in that it is generated out of the Father, so that it is the *Heart* of the Father in his powers.

42. And being *generated*, it is another person than the Father is; for the Father is the *power* and the kingdom, and the Son is the *light* and the splendour in the Father, and the Holy Ghost is the *moving* or *exit* out of the powers of the Father and of the Son, and formeth, figureth, *frameth* and imageth all.

46. Now if a man should say the Son of God were an image, circumscriptive or measurable like the sun, then the three Persons would be only in that place where the Son is, and his splendour or *shining* would be without or beyond him, and as gone forth from the Son; and the Father would be one, only externally, without or beside the Son, and then the power of the Father, which would be afar off and wide distant from the Son, *would not* generate the Son and Holy Ghost, externally, without and beyond the angelical gates; and so there would be an unalmighty being, externally, without or beside this place of the Son; and, moreover, the Father would be a circumscribed or measurable being.

47. Which is *not* so: But the Father everywhere generateth the Son out of all his powers, and the Holy Ghost goeth everywhere forth from the Father and the Son, and so *there is* but ONE only God in one being, with three distinct persons.

48. Of which you have a similitude in the precious gold ore, or a goldstone unseparated. First there is the matter, that is, the *Salitter* and *Mercurius*, which is the *mother* or the whole stone, which generateth the gold everywhere in the whole *stone*; and in the gold is the glorious power or virtue of the stone.

51. Thus also is the place or space in the *centre* or midst of the angelical gates a more pleasant, more gracious, amiable and blessed place to the Father, wherein his Son and Heart is generated in the most richly and fully loving manner, and wherein the Holy Ghost goeth forth from the Father and the Son in the most richly and fully loving manner.

52. Thus you have the right ground of this Mystery, and you *ought not* to think that the Son of God was generated of the Father at *once*, at a *certain time*, as one that hath a beginning, and that he standeth now as a *king*, and would be worshipped.

53. No; this would *not* be an eternal Son, but one that had a beginning, and was under, beneath or *inferior* to the Father that had generated him.

54. *Neither* would he be all-knowing, for he could not know how it was before his Father had generated him.

55. But the Son is generated *continually* from eternity unto eternity, and shineth continually from eternity into the powers of the Father again, whereby the powers of the Father are always from eternity to eternity *continually* impregnated with the Son, and generate him continually.

56. Out of which the Holy Ghost *continually* existeth from eternity to eternity, and so continually from eternity to eternity goeth forth from the Father and the Son, and hath neither beginning nor end.

70. But *here* I will shew thee the right Mystery. Behold, the sun is the heart of all powers in this world, and is compacted, framed or composed out of all the powers of the stars, it *re-enlighteneth* all the stars, and all the powers in this world, and all powers grow *active*, operative or qualifying in its power.

[**71.** *"Understand it magically: For it is a mirror, looking-glass, or similitude of the eternal world."*]

The Eighth Chapter

OF THE WHOLE CORPUS OR BODY OF AN ANGELICAL KINGDOM.

Question.

21. Now the question is, What in heaven is the wrath of God? And whether God be angry in himself; or how is God moved to anger?

Answer.

Here there are chiefly *seven* sorts of qualities or circumstances to be observed.

I. Of the First Species or Circumstance.

22. First: In the divine power there is, hidden in secret, the astringent quality, which is a quality of the *kernel*, pith or hidden being, a sharp compaction or penetration in the *Salitter*, very sharp and harsh or astringent, which *generates* hardness, and also coldness; and when the astringent quality is *kindled* it generateth a sharpness like unto *salt*.

II. Of the Second Species or Circumstance.

32. The Second quality, or second spirit of God in the divine *Salitter*, or in the divine power, is the *sweet* quality, which worketh in the astringent, and mitigateth the astringent, so that it is altogether lovely, pleasant and mild or meek.

33. For it is the *overcoming* of the astringent quality, and is the very source or *fountain* of the mercy of God, which overcometh the wrath, whereby the astringent harsh source is *mollified*, and God's mercy riseth up.

III. Of the Third Circumstance or Species.

44. The Third quality, or the third spirit of God in the Father's power, is the bitter quality; which is a penetrating or *forcing* of the sweet and the astringent or harsh qualities, and which is *trembling*, penetrating and rising up.

48. The bitter quality is the first spirit from whence mobility taketh its original, whence the *life* becometh stirring, and is well called *Cor* or the heart, for it is the trembling, shivering, elevating, penetrating spirit, a triumphing or joy, an elevating source of *laughing*; in the sweet quality the bitter is mollified, so that it becometh very richly loving and joyful.

49. But if it be moved, elevated and kindled too much, then it kindleth the sweet and the astringent or harsh qualities, and is like a tearing, stinging and *burning* poison, as when a man is tormented with a raging plague-sore, which maketh him *cry out* for woe and misery.

IV. Of the Fourth Circumstance or Species.

59. The Fourth quality, or the fourth fountain-spirit in the divine power of God the Father, is the heat, which is the true *beginning* of life, and also the true *spirit* of life.

60. The astringent or harsh and sour quality, and the sweet, are the *Salitter*, which belongeth to the *body*, out of which the body is framed.

61. For coldness and hardness stand in the astringent quality, and are a *contraction* and drying; and in the *sweet* quality stand the water, and the light or shining-ness, and the whole matter of the body.

62. And the bitter quality is the *separation* and forming, and the heat is the spirit, or the kindling of the life, whereby the spirit existeth in the body, which [spirit] springeth or moveth in the whole body, and shineth out from the body, and also maketh the *living motion* in all the qualities of the body.

63. Two things chiefly are to be eyed in *all the qualities*: If you look upon a body you first see the stock or pith, or the kernel of all the qualities, which is framed or *composed* out of all the qualities; for to the body belong the astringent or harsh, sour, sweet, bitter and hot qualities; these qualities being *dried together*, make the body or stock.

The Great Mystery of the Spirit.

64. Now in the body these qualities are *mixed*, as if they all were but *one* quality; yet each quality moveth or boileth in its own power, and so goeth forth.

65. *Each* quality goeth forth from itself into the others, and *toucheth* or stirreth the others, that is, it *affecteth* the others, whereby the other qualities get the will of this quality; that is, they prove the sharpness and spirit of this, as to what *is in it*, and always mix with it continually.

V. Of the Fifth Circumstance or Species.

155. The Fifth quality, or the fifth spirit of God among the seven spirits of God, in the divine power of the Father, is the *gracious, amiable*, blessed, friendly and joyful *love*.

156. Now observe what is the fountain of the *gracious, amiable,* blessed and friendly love of God; observe it exactly, for it is the very pith, marrow or *kernel*.

164. O noble guest! O, *why* didst thou depart from us! O fierceness, wrath and astringency or severity, *thou* art the cause of it! O fierce wrathful devil! O, what hast *thou* done, who hast *sunk down* thyself and thy beautiful bright angels into darkness? Woe, woe for ever!

165. O, was not the gracious, amiable, blessed and fair love in *thee* also? O thou high and lofty-minded devil! Why wouldst thou not be contented? Wert thou not a Cherubim? and was there anything *so* beautiful and bright in heaven as *thou*? For what didst thou seek? Wouldst thou be the whole or *total* God? Didst thou not know that thou wert a creature, and hadst *not* the fan and casting-shovel in thy own hand or power?

166. O, *why* do I pity thee, thou stinking goat? O thou cursed stinking devil! how hast *thou* spoiled us? How wilt thou excuse thyself? What wilt thou *object* to me?

Objection.

167. Thou sayest, if thy fall had not been, man would never have been thought of.

Answer.

O thou lying devil! Though that should be true, yet the *Salitter* out of which man is made (which is also from eternity, as well as *that* out of which thou art made), had stood in *eternal joy* and bright glory, and had likewise risen up in God, and had tasted of the *gracious*, amiable, blessed love in the seven spirits of God, and enjoyed the heavenly joy.

The Ninth Chapter

OF THE GRACIOUS, AMIABLE, BLESSED, FRIENDLY AND MERCIFUL LOVE OF GOD.

21. *Now observe,* The gracious, amiable, blessed love, which is the *fifth* fountain-spirit in the divine power, is the *hidden* source, fountain or quality which the corporeal being *cannot* comprehend or apprehend, *but* only when it riseth up in the body, and *then* the body triumpheth therein, and behaveth itself friendly, lovely and *courteously*; for that quality or spirit belongeth *not* to the imaging or *framing* of a body, but riseth up in the body, as a *flower* springeth up out of the earth.

22. Now this fountain-spirit taketh its original at *first* out of the sweet quality of the water.

Observe:

74. The seven spirits of God, in their circumference and *space*, contain or comprehend heaven and this world; also the *wide breadth and* *depth* without and beyond the heavens, even above and beneath the world, and in the world, yea *the whole Father*, who hath neither beginning nor end.

75. They contain also *all* the *creatures* both in heaven and in this world; and all the creatures in heaven and in this world are imaged, fashioned or framed out of these spirits, and live in them as in their own *propriety*.

76. Their life and their *reason* is generated in them in such a manner as the divine being is generated, and also in the *same* power.

77. Out of and from the same *body* of the seven spirits of God are *all things* made and produced, all angels, all devils, the heaven, the earth, the stars, the elements, men, beasts, fowls, fishes; all worms, wood trees, also stones, herbs and grass, and *all* whatsoever is.

The Tenth Chapter

OF THE SIXTH QUALIFYING OR FOUNTAIN SPIRIT
IN THE DIVINE POWER.

1. The Sixth qualifying or fountain spirit in the divine power is the sound, tone, tune or noise, wherein all soundeth and tuneth; whence ensued *speech*, language, and the *distinction* of everything, as also the ringing melody and *singing* of the holy angels, and therein consisteth the forming or framing of all *colours*, beauty and ornament, as also the heavenly *joyfulness*.

Question.
2. But thou wilt ask, What is the tone or sound? Or how taketh this spirit its source and original?

Answer.
3. *All* the *seven spirits* are generated one in another, the one continually generateth the other, *not one* of them is the first, nor is any one of them the last; for the last generateth as well the first as the second, third, fourth, and so on to the last.

4. But why one is called the *first*, another the *second*, and so *on*, that is in respect to that which is the first in order to the imaging, framing and *forming* of a creature.

5. For all the seven are *equally* eternal, and none of them hath either beginning or end; and therefore, in that the seven qualities are continually *generating* one another, and that none is without the other, it followeth that there is ONE *Only Eternal Almighty* GOD.

31. But here thou must know that *one* spirit *alone* can not generate another, neither can *two* of them do it, but the birth of a spirit standeth in the operation of *all* the *seven* spirits, *six* of them always generate the *seventh*, and so if *one* of them were not, then the *others* would not be either.

32. But that I sometimes take only two or three to the nativity or birth of a spirit, I do that because of my *own weakness*, for in my corrupted brain I cannot bear them all seven at *once* in their perfection.

33. I see them *all seven* very well, but when I speculate into them, then the spirit riseth up in the *middlemost* fountain or well-spring, where the spirit of life generateth itself, which goeth now *upwards*, now *downwards*, it cannot apprehend all the seven spirits in *one* thought, or at once, but only in *part*.

34. Every spirit hath its *own* quality or source, though indeed it is generated of the others; and so it is with the *apprehension* of man; he hath indeed the fountain of all seven spirits *in* him, but in what quality or fountain soever the spirit riseth up, the qualifying or fountain spirit *thereof*, wherein that same spirit is most *strongly* imaged, is that [one] which he comprehendeth most sharply in *that* rising up.

35. For even in the divine power one spirit, in its rising up, doth *not go* through all the spirits equally *at once*; for when it riseth up, then indeed it toucheth or *stirreth* them all at once, but it is caught in its rising up, so that it must lay down its stateliness and pomp, and not *triumph over all the seven*.

[**36.** "It is the being or substance of the senses and thoughts, otherwise, if a thought through the centre of nature could penetrate all the forms, then it were free from the band of nature."]

45. I *have read* the writings of very high masters, hoping to find therein the ground and true depth; but I have found nothing, but a *half dead* spirit, which in anxiety travaileth and laboureth for health, and yet, because of its great weakness, *cannot* attain perfect power.

46. Thus I stand yet as an anxious woman in travail, and seek *perfect* refreshing, but find only the scent or smell or savour in its rising up, wherein the spirit examineth what power *sticketh* in the true cordial, and in the meanwhile refresheth itself in its sickness with that *perfect smell* or savour, till the true *Samaritan* doth come, who will dress and bind up its wounds and heal it, and bring it to the eternal *inn* or lodging, then shall it enjoy the *perfect taste.*

47. This *herb*, which I mean here, from whose fragrancy my spirit taketh its refreshing, every country ploughman doth not know it, *nor* every doctor, the one is as ignorant of it as the other; it groweth indeed in *every* garden, but in many it is quite spoiled and bad: for the quality of the soil or ground is in *fault.* And therefore men do not know it, nay the *children of this Mystery* do hardly know it; although this knowledge hath been very rare, dear and precious, from the beginning of the world to this *time.*

48. Though in many men a source or fountain and quality hath risen up, but then suddenly pride pressed after it, and *spoiled* all; whereupon it [pride] was loath to write it down in its mother-tongue; it supposed that was *too* childish a thing to do, it must shew it in a *deeper* language, that the world should see that it is manly; and for its *advantage* it kept it [the source or fountain and quality] in secret, and *daubed* it with deep strange names, that men might not know it; such a *beast* is the devil's disease of pride.

Question.

74. Thou askest, *How* can a man quench this kindled fire?

Answer.

75. Hearken, thou hast the *sweet* water in thee, pour that into the fire, and then the fire goeth out: If thou *lettest* it burn, then it consumeth in thee the sap that is in all the seven qualifying or fountain spirits, so that thou wilt become dry.

76. *When that is done, then thou art a hellish fire-brand, and a billet or faggot to lay upon the hellish fire, and then there is no remedy for thee eternally.*

81. But thou must know, that thou, in the government of thy mind, art *thine own* lord and master, there will rise up *no* fire to thee in the circle or whole circumference of thy body and spirit, *unless* thou awakenest it *thyself*.

82. It is true that all thy spirits spring and move in thee, and rise up in thee, and indeed *always* one spirit hath *more* power in thee than [in] another [man].

83. For if the government of the spirits were the same in one man as in another, then we should *all* have *one* will and form; but all seven are in *the power* of thy compacted incorporated spirit, which spirit is the SOUL.

[84. *"It hath in it the* first Principle; *the spirit of the soul hath the* second; *and the astral or starry spirit in the elements hath the* third, *viz. this world."*]

103. *Yea, God is so near thee, that the birth or geniture of the Holy Trinity is done or wrought even in thy heart, yea, all the three Persons are generated in thy heart, even God the Father, Son, and Holy Ghost.*

104. Now when I write here concerning the midst or *centre*, that the fountain of divine birth or geniture is in the midst or centre, the meaning is *not* that in heaven there is a peculiar or *several* place, or a peculiar *several* body, wherein the fire of the divine life riseth up, out of which the seven spirits of God go forth into the *whole deep* of the Father.

105. No; but I speak in a corporeal or angelical or human way that the

Reader may the better understand it, in such a manner as the angelical creatures were imaged or framed, and as it is in God everywhere *universally*.

106. For thou canst not nominate any place, either in heaven or in this world, wherein the divine birth or geniture is *not thus*, be it in an angel, or in a holy man, or anywhere else.

107. Wheresoever one qualifying or fountain spirit in the divine power is *touched* or stirred, let the place be where it will or the thing what it will (*except* in the devils, and all wicked, damned men), there is the fountain of the divine birth or geniture directly at hand, and there *already* are all the seven qualifying or fountain spirits of God.

108. As when thou wouldst make a spacious, *creaturely*, circumscribed circle, and hadst the whole Deity peculiarly *apart* therein. Just as the Deity is generated in a creature, so it is also in the whole deep of the Father in all places and parts thereof, and in all *things*.

The Eleventh Chapter

OF THE SEVENTH QUALIFYING OR FOUNTAIN SPIRIT
IN THE DIVINE POWER.

1. The Seventh spirit of God in the divine power is the *corpus* or body, which is generated out of the other *six* spirits, wherein *all* heavenly figures subsist, and wherein all things image and form themselves, and wherein all *beauty* and joy rise up.

2. This is the very spirit of nature, yea *nature itself*, wherein apprehensibility or comprehensibility consisteth, and wherein all creatures are formed in heaven and on earth. Yea *heaven* itself is therein formed; and all *naturality* in the whole God consisteth in *this* spirit.

3. If it were not for this spirit there would be neither angel nor man, and God would be an *unsearchable* being, subsisting *only* in an unsearchable power.

Question
4. Now the question is: How is this form? Or in what manner is this so?

Answer

If thou art a rational mercurial spirit, which *presseth* through all the seven spirits of God, and beholdeth, proveth and examineth them, how they are, then thou wilt, by the *explanation* of this seventh spirit, conceive and understand the *operation* and the *being* of the whole Deity, and apprehend it in thy sense or mind.

11. Behold, all the seven spirits of God are generated alike together at once; none of them is the first, and none of them is the last; but we must have an eye to the kernel, and consider how the divine birth or *geniture* riseth up, otherwise man understandeth it not.

12. For the creatures cannot comprehend *at once* all the seven spirits, one in another, but they look upon them; but when one spirit is touched or stirred, then that toucheth or stirreth all the others, and then the birth or geniture standeth in full power.

13. Therefore it hath a beginning *in man*, but none *in God*; and therefore I must also write in a *creaturely* manner, or else thou *canst not* understand it.

14. Behold, without the flash all the seven spirits were a dark valley, but when the *flash* riseth up between the astringent and bitter qualities, in the heat, then it becometh *shining* in the sweet water, and in the flames of the heat it becometh bitter, and triumphing and living, and in the astringent it becometh corporeal, dry and *bright*.

15. Now these four spirits move themselves in the flash, for all the four become living therein, and so now the power of these four riseth up in the flash, as if the *life* did rise up, and the *power* which is risen up in the flash is the love, which is the *fifth spirit*.

16. That power moveth so very pleasantly and amiably in the flash, as if a dead spirit did become living, and was suddenly in a moment set into great clarity or *brightness*.

17. Now in this moving one power toucheth or stirreth another: First the astringent beateth or striketh, and the heat maketh in that beating or stroke a *clear* ringing sound, and the bitter power divideth the ringing, and the water maketh it mild and soft, and mitigateth it; and this is *the sixth spirit*.

18. Now the tone in all the *five* spirits riseth up like a melodious pleasant music, and remaineth so standing; for the astringent quality exsiccateth it or drieth it up.

19. So now, in the same sound *that is gone forth* (which now subsisteth, being dried) is the power of *all the six* qualifying or fountain spirits, and it is as it were the *seed* of the other six spirits, which they have there compacted or incorporated together, and made one spirit thereof, and which hath the quality of *all* the spirits: and that is *the seventh spirit of God* in the divine power.

22. The seven spirits are the *father* of the light, and the light is their son, which they always continually generate thus from eternity to eternity, and the light enlighteneth and always eternally maketh the seven spirits living and joyful, for they all receive their rising and *life* in the power of light.

23. Again, they all generate the light, and all are together alike the father of the light, and the light generateth no one spirit, but maketh them *all* living and *joyful*, that they always continually stand in the birth.

The Holy Gates.

32. But the *light*, which subsisteth in the midst or centre in all the seven spirits, and wherein standeth the *life* of all the seven spirits, whereby all seven become triumphing and joyful, and wherein the heavenly *joyfulness* rises up:

33. That is *that* which all the seven spirits generate, and that is the *son* of all the seven spirits, and the seven spirits are its *father*, which generate the light; and the light generateth in them the *life*; and the *light* is the heart of the seven spirits.

34. *This light is the true Son of God, whom we Christians worship and honour, as the second Person in the Holy Trinity.*

85. The seventh qualifying or fountain spirit of God is the qualifying or fountain spirit of *nature*: for the *other* six do generate the seventh; and the seventh, when it is generated, is then as it were the *mother* of the seven, which encompasseth the other six, and generateth them again: for the *corporeal* and *natural* being consisteth in the seventh.

102. Now as that quality is which is *strongest*, so the body of the fruit is imaged, and the colours also; in this striving or wrestling the *Deity* formeth itself into infinite and unsearchable variety of kinds and manners of images or ideas.

103. For the seven spirits are the *seven* head sources or springs, and when *Mercurius* riseth up therein, that stirreth all, and the bitter quality moveth it, and *distinguisheth* it, and the astringent *drieth* it up.

[**104.** "Nature *and the* Ternary *are not one and the same; they are distinct, though the Ternary dwelleth in nature, but unapprehended, and yet is an eternal band, as is plainly unfolded in our second and third books.*"]

139. But the cold and *half*-dead body doth not *always* understand this fight of the soul: The body doth not know how it is with it, but is heavy and anxious; it goeth from one room or *business* to another; and from one place to another; it seeketh for ease and rest.

140. When it cometh thither, where it *would be*, yet it findeth no such thing; then doubtings and unbelief fall in between and come upon it; sometimes it seems to it as if God had *quite* cast it off; but it doth *not* understand the fight of the spirit, how the same is sometimes down, and sometimes gets aloft.

141. What vehement and furious war and fight there is between the *hellish* quality and the *heavenly*, which fire the devils *blow up*, and the holy angels *quench* it, I leave to every holy soul to consider of.

142. Thou must know that I write not here as a story or history, as if it were *related* to me from another, but I must continually stand in that combat or battle, and I find it to be full of heavy strivings, wherein I am often struck down to the ground, as well as all other men.

143. But for the sake of the violent fight, and for the sake of the *earnestness* which we have together, this revelation hath been given me, and the vehement driving or impulse to bring it so to pass as to set all this down on *paper*.

144. But what the total sequel is, which may follow upon and after this, I do not *fully* know: Only sometimes, future Mysteries in the depth are shewn to me.

145. For when the flash riseth up in the centre, one seeth through and through, but cannot well apprehend or lay hold on it; for it happeneth to such a one as when there is a tempest of *lightning*, where the flash of fire openeth itself, and suddenly vanisheth.

146. So it goes also in the soul, when it presseth or breaks quite through in its flight or *combat*, then it beholdeth the *Deity*, as a flash of lightning; but the source, quality or fountain of sins covereth it suddenly again: For the *Old* Adam belongeth to the earth, and doth not, with *this* flesh, belong to the Deity.

The Twelfth Chapter

OF THE NATIVITY AND PROCEEDING FORTH OR DESCENT
OF THE HOLY ANGELS, AS ALSO OF THEIR
GOVERNMENT, ORDER, AND HEAVENLY JOYOUS LIFE.

Observe the Depth.

4. There are seven spirits of God, all these *seven* have moved themselves, and the *light* therein hath moved itself also, and the *spirit*, which goeth forth out of the seven spirits of God, hath moved itself also.

5. Now the Creator intended, according to his *Ternary*, to create three hosts, not one from another, but one *by* another, as in a circle or sphere.

6. Now observe: As the spirits were therein in their moving, boiling or rising up, *so* also were the creatures: In the midst or centre of each host was the *heart* of each host incorporated or compacted together, out of which an angelical or great or chief prince proceeded or came to be.

Question.
28. Why hath God created angel-princes and not made them all *equal*, or alike?

Answer.
29. Behold, *God is the God of order*; and as it is, and as it goeth and moveth in his government in himself, that is, in his birth or geniture, and in his rising up, so also is the *order* of the angels.

30. Now as there are in him *chiefly* seven qualities, whereby the *whole* divine being is driven on, and sheweth itself infinitely in these seven qualities, and yet these seven qualities are the chief or *prime* in the infiniteness, whereby the divine birth or geniture stands eternally in its order unchangeably:

31. And as in the *midst* or centre of the seven spirits of God the heart of life is generated, whence the divine joy riseth up; *thus* also is the order of angels.

Of his Creation.
134. As *Michael* is created according to the quality, manner and property of God the Father, so was *Lucifer* created according to the quality, condition and beauty of God the Son, and was bound to and united with him in love, as a dear son or heart, and his heart also stood

in the *centre* of light, as if he had been God himself; and his beauty or brightness transcended all.

135. For his circumference, conception or chief mother, was the Son of God, and there he stood as a king or prince of God.

136. His court, province, place, region or quarters, wherein he dwelt with his whole army or company, and wherein he is become a *creature*, and which was his kingdom, is the created heaven and this world, *wherein* we dwell with our King JESUS CHRIST.

The Thirteenth Chapter

OF THE TERRIBLE, DOLEFUL, AND LAMENTABLE, MISERABLE FALL OF THE KINGDOM OF *LUCIFER*.

22. But to me is shewn the ladder of *Jacob*, upon which I am climbed up, even into heaven, and have received my ware, to offer for sale: Therefore if any one will climb up after me, let him take heed that he be not drunken, but he must be girt with the sword of the spirit.

23. For he must climb through a horrible deep, a *giddiness* will frequently come into his head; and besides, he must climb through the midst or centre of the kingdom of hell, and there he will feel by experience what a *deal* of scoffings and upbraidings he must endure.

24. In this combat I had many hard trials to my *heart's* grief: My sun was often eclipsed or *extinguished*, but did rise again; and the oftener it was eclipsed or put out, the *brighter* and clearer was its rising again.

44. But the seven spirits, which are in an angel, and which generate the light and understanding, are bound and united with the *whole* God, that they should not qualify any other way, either higher or more vehemently, than God himself; but that there should be one and the same *manner* and way between *them both*.

45. Seeing they are but a part or piece of the whole, and not the whole itself, for God hath therefore created them out of *himself*, that they should qualify, operate or act in such a manner, form and way as God himself doth.

46. But now the qualifying or fountain spirits in *Lucifer* did not so; but they, seeing that they sat in the highest primacy or *rank*, moved themselves so hard and strongly that the spirit which they generated was very fiery, and climbed up in the fountain of the heart, like a proud *damsel* or virgin.

54. But when they elevated themselves in a sharp or strong kindling, then they did *against* nature's right otherwise than God their Father did, and this was a stirring quality or rising up *against,*or contrary to the whole Deity.

55. For they kindled the *Salitter* of the body, and generated a high triumphing son, which in the astringent quality was hard, rugged or rough, dark and cold, and in the sweet was *burning*, bitter and fiery; the tone was a hard *fiery noise*; the love was a lofty *enmity* against God.

56. Here now stood the kindled bride in the seventh nature-spirit, like a *proud beast*; now she supposed she was beyond or above God, nothing was like her now: Love grew *cold*, the Heart of God could not touch it, for there was a *contrary* will or opposition between them. The Heart of God moved very meekly and lovingly, and the heart of the angel moved very darkly, *hard*, cold and fiery.

Now observe:

65. The whole Deity hath in its innermost or beginning birth, in the pith or kernel, a very tart, terrible *sharpness*, in which the astringent quality is a very horrible, tart, hard, dark and cold attraction or drawing together, like *winter*, when there is a fierce, bitter, cold frost, when water is frozen into ice, and besides it is very intolerable.

66. Then think or suppose, if in such a hard winter, when it is so cold, the *sun* should be taken away, what kind of hard frost, and how very rough, *fierce* and hard darkness would it be, wherein no life *could* subsist.

67. After such a manner and kind is the astringent quality in the innermost kernel or pith *in itself*, and to itself alone, without the other qualities *in God*; for the austereness or severity maketh the attraction or drawing together, and fixation or glutinousness of the body, and the hardness drieth it up, so that it subsisteth as a creature.

68. And the bitter quality is a *tearing*, penetrating and cutting bitter quality or soúrce: for it *divideth* and driveth forth from the hard and astringent quality, and maketh the mobility.

69. Between these two qualities is heat generated from its hard and fierce bitter rubbing, tearing and raging, which riseth up in the bitter and hard quality, as a *fierce* wrathful kindling, and presseth quite through, as a *hard* fiery *noise*.

70. From whence existeth the hard tone, and in that rising up or climbing, it is environed and *fixed* in the astringent quality, so that it becometh a body which subsisteth.

85. But if I should describe the Deity in its birth or *geniture* in a small round circle, in the highest depth, then it is *thus:*

In a Similitude.

86. Suppose a WHEEL standing before thee, with seven *wheels* one so made in the other that it could go on *all* sides, forward, backward and cross ways, without need of any turning back or stopping.

87. In its going, that always-one wheel, in its turning about, *generateth* the others, and yet none of them vanish out of sight, but that all seven be visible or in sight.

88. The seven wheels always generating the *naves* in the midst or centre according to their turning about, so that the nave stands always free without alteration or removing, whether the wheels go forward or backward or cross ways or upward or downward.

89. The nave always generating the *spokes*, so that in their turning about they stand right and direct from the *nave* to the *fellies* of the wheel: and yet none of the *spokes* to be out of sight, but still turning about thus one with another, going whithersoever the *wind* driveth it, and that without need of any turning back or *stopping*.

Now observe what I shall inform you in the application of this.

90. The *seven wheels* are the seven spirits of God, the one always generating the others, and are like the turning about of a wheel, which hath seven wheels *one in another*, and the one always wheeleth itself otherwise than the others in its station or position, and the seven wheels are *hooped* round with *fellies*, like a round *globe*.

91. And yet that a man may see all the seven wheels turning round about severally apart, as also the whole *fitness* or compass of the frame, with all its fellies and spokes and naves.

92. The *seven naves* in the midst or centre being as it were *one nave*, which doth fit everywhere in the turning about, and the wheels continually generating these naves, and the naves generating the spokes continually in all the seven wheels, and yet none of the wheels, as also none of the naves, nor any of the fellies or spokes, *to be out of sight*, and as if this wheel had *seven* wheels, and yet were all but *one* wheel, and went always *forward*, whithersoever the wind drove it.

Now behold, and consider:

93. The seven wheels one in another, the one always generating the others, and going on every side, and yet none out of sight, or turning back; these are the *seven* qualifying or fountain *spirits* of God the Father.

94. They generate in the seven wheels in each wheel a nave, and yet there are not seven naves, but *one* only, which fitteth in all the seven wheels: This is the heart or *innermost* body of the wheels, wherein the wheels run about, and that signifieth the *Son* of God.

95. For all the seven spirits of God the Father generate continually in their circle, and that is the Son of all the seven spirits, and all those qualify or *act* in his light, and [the Son] is in the midst or centre of the birth, and *holds together* all the seven spirits of God, and they in their birth turn about therewith thus.

96. That is, they climb either upward or downward, backward or forward, or crossways, and so the Heart of God is *always* in the midst or centre, and fitteth itself to every qualifying or fountain spirit.

97. Thus there is *one* Heart of God, and *not* seven, which is always generated from all the seven, and is the heart and *life* of all the seven.

98. Now the *spokes*, which are always generated from the naves and wheels, and which fit themselves to all the wheels in their turning, and are their root, stay and fastening in which they stand, and out of which they are generated, signify God the *Holy Ghost*, which goeth

forth from the Father and the Son, even as the spokes go out from the nave and wheel, and yet *abide* also *in* the wheel.

99. Now as the spokes are many, and go always about with and in the wheel, so the Holy Ghost is the *workmaster* in the wheel of God, and formeth, imageth and frameth all in the whole or total God.

100. Now this wheel hath seven wheels one in another, and one nave, which fitteth itself to all the seven wheels, and all the seven wheels *turn on that one nave*: Thus God is one God, with seven qualifying or fountain spirits one in another, where always one generateth the others, and yet is but one God, just as these seven wheels are but *one* wheel.

105. As the seven wheels turn about upon one nave, as upon their heart, which *holds* them, and they hold the nave, so the seven spirits generate the heart, and the *heart* holds the seven spirits, and so there arise *voices*, and *divine* joyfulness of hearty loving and kissing.

106. For when the spirits with their light move or boil, turn about and rise one in another, then the life is *always* generated; for one spirit always affordeth to the others its taste or relish, that is, it is *affected* by the others.

107. Thus one tasteth and feeleth another, and in the sound one heareth another, and the tone presseth forth from all the seven spirits *towards* the heart, and riseth up in the heart in the flash of the light, and then rise up the voices and *joyfulness* of the Son of God; and all the seven spirits triumph and rejoice in the Heart of God, each according to its quality.

108. For in the light in the *sweet* water all astringency and hardness and bitterness and heat are mitigated and made pleasant, and so there is in the seven spirits nothing else but a *pleasant* striving, struggling and wonderful generating, like a divine holy sport or scene of God.

109. But their sharp or tart birth, of which I have written above, abideth *hidden* as a kernel, for it becometh mitigated by the light and the sweet water.

The Fourteenth Chapter

HOW *LUCIFER*, WHO WAS THE MOST BEAUTIFUL
ANGEL IN HEAVEN, IS BECOME THE MOST HORRIBLE DEVIL.

60. *Sin* hath *seven* kinds, forms, species or sorts; among which there are *four* special well-springs or sources: And the *eighth* kind or sort is the *house of death*.

Now observe:

61. The *seven forms* are the seven qualifying or fountain spirits of the body; when these are kindled each spirit generateth a special or particular enmity against God.

62. Out of these seven are generated *other four* new sons, and they together are the *new god*, which is wholly against the *old God*, as two professed armies of enemies, which have sworn eternal enmity one against the other.

The first Son is PRIDE. *The second Son is* COVETOUSNESS. *The third Son is* ENVY. *The fourth Son is* WRATH.

The Fifteenth Chapter

OF THE *THIRD* SPECIES, KIND OR FORM AND
MANNER OF *SIN's* BEGINNING IN *LUCIFER*.

43. Now when I write of the animated *soulish spirit*, then you must exactly know *what it is*, or *how it is*, else thou wilt read this birth or geniture in vain, and it will happen to thee as it did to the wise

Heathen, who climbed up to the very face or countenance of God, but could not *see* it.

44. The *spirit of the soul* is very much more subtle, and more incomprehensible than the body, or the seven qualifying or fountain spirits, which hold, retain and form the body; for it goeth forth from the seven spirits, as God the Holy Ghost goeth forth from the Father and the Son.

45. The seven qualifying or fountain spirits have their compacted or incorporated body out of nature, that is, out of the seventh nature-spirit in the *divine* power; which in this book I call *the Salitter of God*, or the *Comprehensibility*, wherein the heavenly figures or shapes arise.

46. And that is *a spirit*, as all the rest of the seven spirits are, only the other six are an incomprehensible being therein; for the divine power generateth itself in the comprehensibility of the seventh nature-spirit, as it were hidden or concealed, and incomprehensible to the creatures.

47. But the animated or *soulish* spirit generateth itself in the heart, out of or from the seven qualifying or fountain spirits, in that manner as the Son of God is generated, and keepeth its seat in the heart, and goeth forth from that *seat* in the divine power, as the Holy Ghost from the Father and the Son; for it hath the same subtleness as the Holy Spirit of God, and it uniteth, qualifieth or operateth with God the Holy Ghost.

48. When the animated or soulish spirit goeth forth out of the body, then it is *one* thing with the hidden Deity, and is together the midst or centre in the imaging or framing of a thing in nature, as God the Holy Ghost himself is.

49. An example whereof you have in this: as when a *carpenter* will build a curious house or artificial piece of architecture, or when any other *artist* goeth about the making of some artificial work, the *hands*, which signify *nature*, cannot be the first that begin the work: but the seven spirits are the first workmasters about it, and the animated or soulish spirit sheweth to the seven spirits the form, figure or shape of it.

50. Then the seven spirits image or frame it, and make it comprehensible, and then the hands *first* begin to fall to work, to make the structure according to the image or frame contrived: For a work must be first brought to the sense, before you can make it.

The Sixteenth Chapter

OF THE *SEVENTH* SPECIES, KIND, FORM, OR MANNER
OF SIN'S *BEGINNING* IN LUCIFER AND HIS ANGELS.

6. Now the seventh form, or the seventh spirit in the divine power, is *nature*, or the issue or *exit* from the other six. For the astringent quality attracteth the *Salliter* together, or the fabric or product of all the six spirits, even as a magnet or loadstone attracteth to itself the *Salitter* of the iron; and when it is attracted together, then it is a *comprehensibility*, in which the six spirits of God qualify, act or operate in an *incomprehensible* way or manner.

7. This seventh spirit hath a colour and condition or kind of its own, as all the other spirits have; for it is the *body* of all the spirits, wherein they generate themselves as in a body: Also out of this spirit all *figures*, shapes and forms are imaged or fashioned; moreover, the angels also are created out of it, and *all naturality standeth therein*.

8. And *this spirit* is always generated from the six, and subsisteth always *continually*, and is never missing or wanting, nor doth ever pass away, and it again continually generateth the six; for the other six are in this seventh as in a mother, enclosed or encompassed; and they receive their nourishment, power and strength *always* in their mother's body or womb.

9. For the seventh spirit is the *body*, and the other six are the *life*, and in the middle centre is the heart of *light*, which the seven spirits continually generate as a light of life; and that light is their son; and the welling out or penetration through all the spirits expandeth itself aloft in the heart, in the exit or rising up of the light.

10. And this is the spirit of all the seven spirits, that goeth forth out of the heart of God, which there, in the seventh spirit, formeth and frameth all, and wherein the qualifying or fountain spirits, with their love-wrestling, shew themselves endlessly.

11. For the Deity is like a wheel, which with its *fellies* and *spokes*, and with all the *naves*, turneth about, and is fellied together, as seven wheels, so that it can go any way, forward, backward, downward, upward and crossways, without turning back.

12. Whereas yet always the form of all the seven *wheels*, and the one only *nave* in the centre of all the wheels, is fully in sight, and so it is not understood how the wheel is made; but the wheel always appears more and more *wonderful* and marvellous, with its rising up, and yet abideth also in its own place.

13. In such a manner the Deity is continually generated, and never passeth away, or ceaseth or vanisheth out of sight; and in this manner also is the *life* in angels and men continually generated.

14. According to the moving of the seven spirits of God the figures and creatures of the *transitoriness* are *formed*, but not thus generated; though indeed the birth or geniture of all the seven spirits sheweth itself therein, yet their quality standeth only in the seventh nature-spirit, which the other six spirits do form, figure, frame, *alter* and *change*, according to their *wrestling* and rising up.

15. Therefore also the figures, and *transitory* forms and creatures, are changed according to the condition of the *seventh* nature-spirit, in which they rise up.

110. The spirit alone understandeth this *hidden* secret, which spirit must fight daily and hourly with the *devil*, the outward flesh *cannot* comprehend it; also the astral spirits in man cannot understand it, neither is it comprehended by man at all, unless the animated or soulish spirit unite, qualify and operate with the *innermost* birth or geniture in nature, in the centre, where the light of God is set opposite against the devil's kingdom, that is, in the third birth or geniture, in the *nature* of this world.

111. When it uniteth, qualifieth or operateth with God in *this seat*, then the animated or soulish spirit carrieth it into the *astral*; for the astral must in this place fight hourly with the devil.

112. For the devil *hath* power in the outermost birth or geniture of man, for his seat is there. [This seat is] the murderous den of perdition, and the house of misery and *woe*, wherein the devil *whetteth* the sting of death, and through his animated or *soulish* spirit he reacheth in into the heart of man, in man's outermost birth or geniture.

113. But when the astral spirits are *enlightened* from the animated or soulish spirit, which in the light uniteth with God, then they grow *fervent*, and very longing and desirous of the light. On the other hand, the animated or soulish spirit of the devil, which ruleth in the outermost birth or geniture of man, is very terrible and angry, and of a very contrary or *opposite* will.

114. And then there riseth up the striving or *fighting fire* in man, just as it rose up in heaven with *Michael* and *Lucifer*, and so the poor soul comes to be miserably crushed, *stretched*, tormented and put upon the rack.

115. But if it getteth the victory, then it bringeth with its piercing penetration its light and knowledge into the outermost birth or geniture of man; for it presseth back with force through the seven spirits of nature, which here I call the astral spirits, and governeth in the council [or counsel] of reason.

118. Now this birth of the *flesh* is *not* the mansion-house of the soul, but in its strife the soul goeth in with its light into the *divine* power, and fighteth against the murder of the devil.

119. On the other hand, the devil with his poison shooteth and *darteth* at the seven qualifying or fountain spirits which generate the soul, intending to destroy and to *kindle* them, that thereby he may get the whole body for his own propriety.

120. Now if the soul would willingly bring its light and knowledge into the *human* mind, then it must fight and strive hard and stoutly, and yet hath a very *narrow* passage to enter in at; it will often be knocked down by the devil, but it must stand to it here, like a *champion* in the battle. And if it now gets the *victory*, then it hath conquered the devil; but if the devil prevails and gets the better, then the soul is *captivated.*

121. But seeing the fleshly birth or geniture is not the soul's *own* proper house, and that it cannot possess it as an *inheritance,* as the devil doth, therefore the fight and the battle lasteth as long as the house of flesh lasteth.

122. But if the house of flesh be once destroyed, and that the soul is not *yet* conquered or vanquished in its house, but is free and unimprisoned, then the fight is *ended,* and the devil must be gone from this spirit *eternally.*

123. Therefore this is a very difficult *article* to be understood; nay, it cannot be understood at all, except by experience in *this* fight. Though I should write *many* books thereof, yet thou wouldst understand *nothing* of it, unless thy spirit stand in *such* a birth or geniture, and that the knowledge be generated in thyself; otherwise thou canst neither comprehend *nor believe* it.

The Seventeenth Chapter

OF THE LAMENTABLE AND MISERABLE STATE AND CONDITION
OF THE CORRUPT PERISHED NATURE, AND ORIGINAL OF THE
FOUR ELEMENTS, INSTEAD OF THE HOLY GOVERNMENT OF GOD.

30. The outward comprehensibility or palpability in the whole nature of this world, and of all things which are therein, standeth all in the *wrath-fire* of God, for it is become thus through the kindling of nature; and lord *Lucifer* with his angels hath his dwelling now in the same outward birth or geniture which standeth in the wrath-fire.

31. But now the Deity is *not so separated* from the outward birth or geniture, as if they were *two* things in this world; if so, man could have *no hope*, and then this world did not stand in the power and love of God.

32. But the Deity *is* in the outward birth, hidden, and hath the fan or casting shovel in its hand, and will one day cast the chaff and the kindled *Salitter* upon a heap, and will draw away from it its inward birth or geniture, and give them to lord *Lucifer* and his *crew* of followers for an eternal house.

33. In the *meanwhile* lord *Lucifer* must lie *captive* and imprisoned in the outermost birth in the nature of this world, in the *kindled* wrath-fire; and therein he hath great power, and can reach into the *heart* of all creatures with his animated or soulish spirit in the outermost birth or geniture, which standeth in the wrath-fire.

The Eighteenth Chapter

OF THE CREATION OF HEAVEN AND EARTH; AND OF THE FIRST DAY.

2. But because at that time, when God created heaven and earth, there was *yet no man* who saw it, therefore it may be concluded that *Adam* before his fall, while he was yet in the deep knowledge of God, knew it in the spirit.

3. But yet when he fell, and was set into the *outward* birth or geniture, he knew it no more, but kept it in remembrance, only as a dark and veiled story; and this he left to his posterity.

19. So now, seeing every man is as the whole house of this world, therefore all his qualifying or fountain spirits love the *kernel*, or the best thing that is in the corrupted nature, and that they use for the defence, protection and maintenance of themselves.

20. But the innermost kernel, which is the Deity, that they can nowhere comprehend, for the *wrath* of the fire lieth before it, as a strong wall, *and this wall must be broken down with a very strong storm or assault, if the astral spirits will see into it.* But the door standeth open to the animated or soulish spirit, for it [the animated or soulish spirit] is withheld by nothing, but is as God himself is, in his innermost birth or geniture.

Now then it might be asked, How then shall I understand myself in or according to the three-fold birth or geniture in nature?

The depth!

21. Behold, the *first*, innermost and deepest birth or geniture standeth in the centre, and is the *heart* of the Deity, which is generated by the qualifying or fountain spirits of God; and this birth or geniture is the *light*, which yet, though it be generated out of the qualifying or fountain spirits, no qualifying or fountain spirit of itself alone can comprehend, but every qualifying or fountain spirit comprehendeth only its own in-standing, innate place or seat in the light; but all the seven spirits jointly together comprehend the whole light, for they are the father of the light.

88. Had not our philosophers and doctors always played upon the fiddle of pride, but had played on the *musical instrument* of the prophets and apostles, there would have been far another knowledge and *philosophy* in the world.

89. Concerning which, in regard of my imbecility, want of literature or learning and study, as also the slowness and dulness of my *tongue*, I am very *insufficient*, but not so simple in the knowledge. Only I cannot deliver it in profound language, and in the *ornament* of eloquence, but I rest contented with my gift I have received, and am a *philosopher among the simple*.

138. But it must *not* so be understood as if the Deity were *separated* from nature; no, but they are as body and soul: *Nature* is the body and the *heart of God* is the soul.

Now a man might ask, What kind of light then was it that was kindled? Was it the sun and stars?

139. No, the sun and stars were *first* created but on the fourth day, out of *that* very light: There was a light arisen in the seven spirits of nature which had no peculiar distinct *seat* or place, but did shine everywhere all over, but was *not bright* like the sun, but like an azure blue and light, according to the kind and manner of the qualifying or fountain spirits; till afterwards the right creation and kindling of the *fire* in the water, in the astringent spirit, followed, *viz.* the sun.

The Nineteenth Chapter

CONCERNING THE *CREATED HEAVEN*, AND THE FORM
OF THE *EARTH*, AND OF THE *WATER*,
AS ALSO CONCERNING *LIGHT* AND *DARKNESS*.

12. But the greatness of the triumphing that was in the spirit I *cannot express*, either in speaking or writing; neither can it be compared to anything, but to *that* wherein the life is generated in the midst of death, and it is *like* the resurrection from the dead.

13. In this light my spirit suddenly saw through all, and *in* and *by* all the creatures, even in herbs and grass it knew God, who he is, and how he is, and what his will is: And suddenly in that light my will was set on by a mighty *impulse*, to describe *the being of God.*

14. But because I could not at once apprehend the *deepest* births of God in their *being*, and comprehend them in my *reason*, there passed almost *twelve* years, before the exact understanding thereof was given me.

15. It was with me as with a young tree that is planted in the ground, and at first is young and *tender*, and flourishing to the eye, especially if it comes on lustily in its growing: But [it] doth not bear fruit at once; and though it blossoms, the blossoms fall off; also many a cold wind, frost and snow pass over it, *before* it comes to any growth and bearing of fruit.

16. So also it went with this spirit: The first fire was but a *seed*, and not a constant lasting light: *Since that time* many a cold wind blew upon it; but the will never extinguished.

Now observe:

24. If thou fixeth thy thoughts concerning heaven, and wouldst fain *conceive* in the mind what it is, and where it is, and how it is, thou *needest* not to swing or cast thy thoughts many thousand miles off, for that place, or that heaven, is *not thy* heaven.

25. And though indeed that is united with thy heaven as *one* body, and so together is *but the one* body of God, yet thou art not in that very place which is become a creature, aloft, many hundred thousand miles off; but thou art in the *heaven* of this world, which containeth also in it a deep, such as is not of any human number (or is not circumscriptive).

26. For the *true heaven* is everywhere, even in that very place where thou standest and goest, and so when thy spirit apprehendeth the innermost birth or geniture of God, and presseth in *through* the astral and fleshly geniture, then it is *clearly* in heaven.

But thou must know,

28. That the place of this world with its innermost birth and geniture uniteth or qualifieth with the heaven aloft *above us,* and so there is one heart, one being, one will, *one God, all in all.*

29. But that the place of this world is not called heaven, and that there is a firmament or fast enclosure between the *upper* heaven above us, hath this understanding or meaning, as followeth.

30. The upper heaven compriseth the two kingdoms, that of *Michael,* and that of *Uriel,* with all the holy angels that are *not fallen* with

Lucifer, and that heaven *continueth* as it was from eternity, before the angels were created.

31. The other heaven is this world, in which *Lucifer* was a king, who kindled the outermost birth or geniture in nature; and that now is the *wrath* of God, and cannot be called God or heaven, but *perdition*.

38. The second birth of this world standeth in the life, for it is the *astral* birth, out of which is generated the *third* and holy birth or geniture, and therein love and wrath *strive* the one with the other.

39. For the second birth standeth in the seven qualifying or fountain spirits of this world, and is in all places and in all the creatures, as also in man: But the Holy Ghost also ruleth and reigneth in the *second birth,* and helpeth to generate the *third* holy birth or geniture.

48. Thou seest in this world nothing but the *deep,* and therein the stars, and the birth or geniture of the elements: Now wilt thou say, God is *not* there? Pray then, what was there in that place *before* the time of the world? Wilt thou say, There was nothing? Then thou speakest *without* reason, for thou must *needs* say that God was there, or else nothing would have come to be there.

49. Now if God was *there* then, who hath thrust him *out* from thence or vanquished him, that he should be there *no* more? But if God is there, then he is indeed in his *heaven,* and, moreover, in his *Trinity*.

56. Neither must thou think that the *Deity* is such a kind of being as is *only* in the upper heaven, nor that the soul, when it departeth from the body, goeth up aloft into the upper heaven many hundred thousand miles off.

57. It *needeth* not do that, but it is set or put into the innermost birth,

and there it is with God, and in God, and with all the holy angels, and
can now be above, and now beneath; it is not *hindered* by anything.

58. For in the innermost birth the upper and nether Deity is *one body*,
and is an open gate: The holy angels converse and walk up and down in
the innermost birth of this world *by* and *with* our King JESUS
CHRIST, as well as in the uppermost world aloft in their quarters,
courts or region.

68. Now, where nothing is, there nothing can come to be: All things
must have a *root*, else nothing can grow: If the *seven spirits of nature* had
not been from eternity, then there would have come to be no angel, no
heaven, also no earth.

69. But the earth is come from the corrupted *Salitter* of the outermost
birth or geniture, which thou canst not deny, when thou lookest on
earth and stones, for then thou must needs say that *death* is therein:
On the other hand also thou must needs say that there is a *life* therein,
otherwise neither gold nor silver, nor any plant, herb, grass or vegetable, could grow therein.

Now one might ask, Are there also all the three births or genitures
therein?

Answer.

70. Yes: the life presseth through death; the *outermost* birth is the
death; the *second* is the life, which standeth in the wrath-fire and in
the love; and the *third* is the holy life.

79. But if thou sayest that there is *no* life in the earth, thou speakest as
one that is *blind*; for thou mayest see plainly that herbs and grass grow
out of it.

80. But if thou sayest it hath but *one* kind of birth or geniture, thou
speakest again also like one that is *blind*; for the herbs and wood which
grow out of it are *not* earth, neither is the *fruit*, which groweth upon a
tree, wood; so also the power and *virtue* of the fruit is *not* God either;

but God is in the centre, in the innermost birth in all the three natural births or genitures, *hiddenly*, but is not known, except *in the spirit of man* alone; also the outermost birth in the fruit doth not comprehend, conceive or contain *him*, but he containeth the outermost birth of the fruit, and formeth it.

130. Thou seest also how the wrath of God lieth hid and resteth in the *outermost birth* of nature, and *cannot* be awakened, unless men *themselves* rouse or awaken it, who with their fleshly birth or geniture qualify, operate or unite with the wrath in the *outermost* birth of nature.

The Twentieth Chapter

OF THE SECOND DAY

20. What good will thy knowledge do thee, if thou wilt not strive and *fight* therein? It is just as if one knew of a great treasure, and would not go for it; but, though he knoweth he might have it, would rather *starve* for hunger in the *bare* knowing of it.

The Twenty-First Chapter

OF THE THIRD DAY.

63. It is *not* so to be understood as that I am *sufficient* enough in these things, but only so far as I am able to comprehend.

64. For the being of God is like a wheel, wherein many wheels are

made *one in another*, upwards, downwards, crossways, and yet they continually turn, all of them together.

65. Which, indeed, when a man beholdeth the *wheel*, he highly marvelleth at it and, in its turning, cannot *at once* learn to conceive and *apprehend* it: But the more he beholdeth the wheel, the more he learneth its form or frame; and the more he learneth, the greater longing he hath to the wheel; for he continually seeth somewhat that is more and more wonderful, so that a man can neither behold it, nor learn it *enough*.

66. Thus I also, what I do not *enough* describe in one place concerning this great Mystery, that you will find in another place; and what I cannot describe in this book, in regard of the largeness of the Mystery, and my incapacity, that you will find in the *others* following.

67. For *this book* is the first sprouting or vegetation of this twig, which springeth or groweth green in its mother, and is *as a child* that is learning to walk, and is not able to run apace at the *first*.

Now observe:

69. The earth hath just such qualities and qualifying or fountain spirits as the deep above the earth or as *heaven* hath, and all of them together belong to one only body; and the whole or *universal* God is that one only *body*. But that thou dost not wholly and fully see and know him, *sins are the cause* thereof, with and by which thou, in this great divine body, liest *shut up* in the dead or mortal *flesh*; and the power or virtue of the *Deity* is *hidden* from thee, even as the marrow in the bones is hidden from the *flesh*.

70. But if thou, in the spirit, breakest through the death of the flesh, then thou seest the hidden God. For as the marrow in the bones penetrateth, presseth or breaketh through and giveth virtue, power and strength to the *flesh*, and yet the flesh cannot comprehend or apprehend the marrow, but only the power and *virtue* thereof, so no more canst thou see the hidden Deity in thy flesh, but thou receivest its *power*, and understandest *therein* that God dwelleth in thee.

71. For the dead or *mortal* flesh belongeth not to the birth of *life*, and therefore cannot receive or conceive the life of the light as a *propriety*; but the life of the light in God riseth up in the dead or mortal flesh, and generateth to itself, from or out of the dead or mortal flesh, *another* heavenly and living body, which knoweth and *understandeth* the light.

72. For this body is but a *husk*, from which the new body groweth — ["*The new body groweth out of the heavenly substantiality in the Word, out of the flesh and blood of Christ, out of the* mystery *of the old body.* "] — as it is with a *grain* of wheat in the earth. The husk or shell *will not rise* again, no more than it doth in the wheat, but will remain *for ever* in death and in hell.

78. Thou must know that all the seven spirits of God are *in* the earth, and generate as they do in heaven: For the earth is God, and God never died; but the outermost birth or geniture is *dead*, in which the wrath resteth, and is reserved for king *Lucifer*, to be a house of death and of darkness, and to be an eternal prison or dungeon.

104. But thou art to know that the *earth* hath all the qualifying or fountain spirits. For through the devil's kindling the spirits of life were incorporated or compacted together also in *death*, and, as it were, captivated, but *not* quite murdered.

105. The *first three*, viz. the astringent, the sweet, and the bitter, belong to the imaging or forming of the body; and therein standeth the mobility, and the *body* or corporeity. And these now have the comprehensibility or palpability, and are the birth of the *outermost* nature.

106. The *other three*, viz. the heat, the love, and the tone, stand in the incomprehensibility, and are generated out of the first three; and this now is the inward birth, wherewith the Deity qualifieth, mixeth or uniteth.

107. If the first three were *not* congealed or benumbed in death they *could* kindle the heat, and then thou wouldst soon see a bright, shining, heavenly body, and thou wouldst see plainly *where* God is.

110. Here thou seest once more how the kingdom of God and the kingdom of hell hang one to the other, as *one* body, and yet the one cannot comprehend the other. For the *second birth*, viz. the heat, light, love, and the sound or tone, is hidden in the outermost, and maketh the outward *moveable*, so that the outward gathereth itself together, and generateth a body.

The Twenty-Second Chapter

OF THE BIRTH OR GENITURE OF THE STARS,
AND CREATION OF THE FOURTH DAY.

1. Here now is begun the describing of the astral birth. It ought well to be observed what the *first title* of this book meaneth, which is thus expressed: The *Day-Spring or Dawning in the East*, or *Morning-Redness in the Rising.* For here will a *very simple* man be able to see and comprehend or apprehend the being of God.

2. The Reader should not make himself blind through his *unbelief* and dull apprehension; for here I bring in the whole or total nature, with all her children, for a *witness* and a demonstration. If thou art rational, then look round about thee, and view thyself; also consider thyself aright, and then thou wilt *soon find* from or out of what spirit I write.

3. For my part, I will obediently perform the command of the spirit, only, have thou a care, and suffer not thyself to be shut out by an open door; for here the gates of knowledge stand open to thee.

18. The spirit hath a long time waited on them, and *importuned* them that they would once open the door, for the *clear day* is at hand; yet they walk up and down in their drunkenness, seeking for the key, when they have it about them, though they *know it not*; and so they go up and down in their proud and covetous drunkenness, always seeking about like the country man for his horse, who all the while he went seeking for him was riding upon the *back* of *that very* horse he looked for.

19. *Thereupon*, saith the spirit of nature, *seeing they will not awake from sleep and open the door, I will therefore do it myself.*

20. What could I, poor, simple *layman*, teach or write of their high art, if it were not given to me by the *spirit* of nature, in whom I live and am? I am in the condition or state of a vulgar or layman, and have no *salary*, wages or pay for this writing: Should I, then, oppose the spirit, that he should not *begin* to open where, and in whom, he pleaseth? *I am not the door*, but an ordinary wooden bolt upon it: Now if the spirit should pluck me out from thence, and fling me into the fire, could I hinder it?

22. Behold! I tell thee a Mystery: so soon as the door is set *wide* open to its angle, all useless, fastnailed, sticking bolts or bars will be *cast away*, for the door will *never* be shut any more at all, but standeth open, and then the *four winds* will go in and out at it.

23. But the *sorcerer* sitteth in the way, and will make many *so* blind that they will not see the door; and then they return home and *say*, There is no door at all, it is a mere fiction. And so they go *thither* no more.

24. Thus men suffer themselves easily to be turned away, and so live in their *drunkenness*.

25. Now when this is done, then the spirit which hath opened the gates is angry, because none will go OUT and IN at its doors any more, and then it flings the door-posts into the abyss, and then there is *no more time* at all. Those that are *within*, remain within; and those that are *without*, remain without. AMEN.

30. After these patriarchs came the *wise Heathen*, who went somewhat *deeper* into the knowledge of nature. And I must needs say, according to the ground of the truth, that they, in their philosophy and knowledge, did come even before the face or countenance of God, and yet could *neither* see nor know him.

31. Man was so altogether *dead* in death, and so bolted up in the outermost birth or geniture in the dead palpability; or else they could have thought, that in this palpability there must *needs be a divine power* hidden in the centre, which had *so* created this palpability, and moreover preserveth, upholdeth and ruleth the same.

32. Indeed they honoured, prayed to, or *worshipped* the sun and stars for gods, but knew not how these were created or came to be, nor out of what they came to be.

42. For thou needest *not* to ask, *Where is God?* Hearken, thou blind man; thou livest in God, and *God is in thee*; and if thou livest holily, then *therein* thou thyself art God. For wheresoever thou lookest, there, is God.

44. Or dost thou think that in or at the time of the creation of this world he *departed* and went away from his seat wherein he did sit from eternity? O no; that *cannot* be, for though he *would* himself do so, *he* cannot do it, for he himself is All: As little as a member of the body can be rent off from itself, so little also can God be *divided*, rent or *separated* from being *everywhere*.

45. But that there are so many formings, figurings or framings in him, is caused by his eternal birth or geniture, which first is threefold, and out of or from that Trinity or Ternary it generateth itself *infinitely*, immeasurably or inconceivably.

65. *But seeing men now, at the end of this time, do listen and long very much after the root of the tree, through which nature sheweth that the time of the discovery of the tree is at hand, therefore the spirit will shew it to them.* And the whole Deity will reveal itself, which is the Day-spring, Dawning, or Morning-redness, and the breaking-forth of the great day of God, in which whatsoever is generated from death to the regeneration of life shall be restored and rise again.

88. You have an *example* of this in gold, and in silver, which you cannot make to be pure or fine gold or silver, unless *it be melted seven times in the fire*. But when that is done, then it remaineth in the middle or *central seat* in the heart of nature, which is the water, sitting in its own quality and *colour*.

102. And now, when it is *almost* made, then it hath its true virtue and colour, and there is nothing wanting except in this, that the spirit cannot elevate itself with its *body* into the light, but must remain to be a dead stone; and though indeed it be of *greater* virtue than other stones, yet the *body* remaineth in death.

103. *And this now is the earthly god of blind men,* which they love and honour, and *leave* the living God, who standeth hidden in the centre, sitting in his seat. For the dead flesh comprehendeth only a *dead god*, and longeth also only after such a dead god. *But it is such a god as hath thrown many men headlong into hell.*

104. Do not take me for an alchymist, for I write only in the *knowledge* of the spirit, and not from experience. Though indeed I could here shew *something* else, *viz.* in *how many* days, and in *what hours*, these things must be prepared; for gold cannot be made in one day, but a whole month is requisite for it.

105. But it is not my purpose to make *any* trial at all of it, because I know not how to *manage* the fire; neither do I know the colours or tinctures of the qualifying or fountain spirits in their outermost birth or geniture, which are *two* great defects; but I know them according to (another or) the regenerate man, which standeth *not* in the palpability.

The Twenty-Third Chapter

OF THE DEEP ABOVE THE EARTH.

3. Many will dare to say, What *manner of God* would that be, whose body, being, and power or virtue, standeth or consisteth in fire, air, water and earth?

4. Behold! thou unapprehensive man, I will shew thee the true *ground* of the Deity. *If* this whole or universal being be not God, *then* thou art not God's image. If he be any other or strange God, then thou hast *no part* in him: For thou art created out of this God, and livest *in* this very God, and this very God continually giveth thee power or virtue, and blessing, also meat and drink, *out of himself*; also all thy knowledge standeth in this God, and when thou *diest*, then thou art *buried* in this God.

15. *But observe here rightly* the earnest and *severe* birth or geniture, out of which the wrath of God, hell, and death, are come to be, which indeed have *been* from eternity in God, but not liable to be kindled or to become predominant.

16. For the whole or total God standeth in *seven* species or kinds, or in a sevenfold form or generating; and if these births or genitures were not, then there would be neither God, nor life, nor angel, nor any creature.

17. And *these* births or genitures have *no beginning*, but have so generated themselves from eternity; and as to this depth, *God himself* *knoweth not what he is: For he knoweth no beginning of himself, also he knoweth not anything that is like himself, as also he knoweth no end of himself.*

18. *These seven* generatings *in all* are *none of them* the first, the second, or the third, or last, but they are all seven, every one of them, both the first, second, third, fourth, and last. Yet I must set them down one after another, according to a *creaturely* way and manner, otherwise thou couldst not understand it: For the *Deity* is as a wheel with seven wheels made one in another, wherein a man seeth *neither* beginning nor end.

45. For they wrestle in the birth or geniture *continually* one with another, like a loving play or scene, and according as the birth or geniture is with the *colours* and taste in the rising up, so also are the *figures* imaged.

46. *And this birth or geniture now is called* GOD *the Father, Son, and Holy Ghost:* Not one of them is the first, and not one of them is the last: though I *make* a distinction, and set the one after the other, yet not one of them is the first or the last, but they have all been from eternity thus seated in the same *equality* of being.

47. I must write *thus* by way of *distinction*, that the Reader may understand it; for I cannot write mere heavenly words, but must write human words. Indeed all is rightly, truly and faithfully described: *But the being of God consisteth only in power, and only the spirit comprehendeth it, and not the dead or mortal flesh.*

49. But now this sharp birth or geniture is the *original* of mobility and of life, as also of the light, from whence existeth the *living and rational spirit*, which distinguisheth, formeth and imageth all in this generating.

50. For the astringent cold birth or geniture is the *beginning* of all things, which quality is astringent, severe, contracting and retentive, and formeth and contracteth together the birth, and maketh the birth thick or solid, so that out of it *nature* cometh to *be*; hence nature and comprehensibility hath its original in the whole body of God.

51. Now *this nature* is as a *dead*, unintellectual being, and standeth or consisteth not in the power of the birth or geniture, but is a body, wherein the power generateth.

52. But it is the body of God, and hath all power as the whole geniture hath, and the generating spirits take their strength and power out of or from the *body* of nature, and continually generate again, and the astringent spirit continually compacteth or draweth together again, and drieth up; and thus the body subsisteth, and the generating spirits also.

64. Thou seest also that nature cannot be *distinguished* from the powers of God, but is all one body.

65. The Deity, that is, the holy power of the heart of God, is generated *in nature*, and so also the Holy Ghost existeth or goeth forth out of the heart of the light *continually*, through all the powers of the Father, and figureth all, and imageth or frameth all.

66. This birth or geniture is now in *three* distinct *parts*, every part being several and *total*, and yet *not one* of them is divided asunder from the others.

78. *Thus there is one God, and three distinct Persons one in another* and not one of them can comprehend, or withhold, or fathom the original of the others, but the *Father* generateth the Son, and the *Son* is the Father's heart, and his love and his light, and is an original of joy, and the *beginning* of all life.

79. And the *Holy Ghost* is the spirit of life, and a former, framer and creator of all things, and a *performer* of the will in God; that hath formed and created out of or from the body, and in the body of the Father, all angels and creatures, and holdeth and formeth all *still*, daily, and is the sharpness and the living spirit of God: *As the Father speaketh or expresseth the Word, out of or from his powers, so the spirit formeth or frameth them.*

83. Thou must know that I do not suck it out from the dead or mortal *reason*, but my spirit qualifieth, mixeth or uniteth with God, and proveth or searcheth the *Deity*, how it is in all its births or genitures in its taste and smell: And I find that the Deity is a very simple, *pure*, meek loving and quiet being; and that the birth of the *Ternary* of God generateth itself very meekly, friendly, lovingly and unanimously, and the *sharpness* of the innermost birth *can never* elevate or swell itself into the meekness of the *Ternary*, but remaineth *hidden* in the deep.

Now thou wilt say to me:
90. *Dost not thou seek after deeper subtlety than we? Thou wilt [wishest to] climb into the most hidden secrets of God, which is not fit for any man to go about. We seek only after human prudence and subtlety, but thou wouldst be equal with God, and know all; how God is in every thing, both in heaven and in hell, in devils, angels and men. Therefore, sure it is not unlawful to seek for a cunning, sharp wit, and after crafty designs, which bring honour, power or authority, and riches.*

A Reply.
91. If thou climbest up *this ladder* on which I climb up into the deep of God, as I have done, then thou hast climbed well: I am not come to this meaning, or to this work and *knowledge*, through my *own* reason, or through my *own* will and purpose; neither have I sought this knowledge, nor so much as knew anything concerning it. I sought only for the *Heart* of God, *therein* to hide myself from the tempestuous storms of the *devil*.

92. But when I gat in thither, then this great, weighty and hard labour was laid upon me, which is, to manifest and *reveal* to the world, and to make known, *the great day of the* LORD; and, seeing men seek and long so eagerly after the *root* of the tree, to reveal to them what the whole tree is, thereby to intimate that it [the present time] is *the Dawning, or Morning-Redness of the Day*, which God hath long ago *decreed* in his council. AMEN.

The Twenty-Fourth Chapter

OF THE INCORPORATING OR COMPACTION OF THE STARS.

1. Now when the *whole body* of nature in the extent, space or circumference of this world was benumbed or *deadened*, as in the hard death, and yet that the life was *hid* therein, thereupon God moved the whole body of the nature of this world on the *fourth day*, and generated the stars from or out of nature, out of the risen light. For the wheel of God's birth or geniture *moved* itself *again*, as it *had done* from eternity.

13. This now is the *sum* or the contents of the astral birth or geniture, of which I here intend to write.

Now it may be asked, What are the stars? or out of what are they come to be?

14. They are the *power* of the seven spirits of God; for when in this world the wrath of God was kindled by the devil, then the *whole house* of this world in nature, or the outermost birth or geniture, was as it were benumbed or *chilled* in death; from whence the *earth* and *stones* are come to be. But when this hard dross or *scum* was driven together into a lump or heap, then the *deep* was cleared. But the deep was very dark, for the light therein was dead in the *wrath*.

28. But that there are so many stars of so manifold different effects and operations is from the *infiniteness*, which is in the efficiency of the seven spirits of God, in one another, which generate themselves infinitely.

31. Behold! the stars are plainly incorporated or *compacted* out of or from God; but thou must understand the difference between the stars and God, for the stars are *not* the heart and the meek pure Deity, which man *is to honour* and worship as God; but they are the innermost and sharpest birth or geniture, wherein all things stand in a wrestling and a *fighting*, wherein the heart of God always generateth itself, and wherein the Holy Ghost *continually* riseth up from the rising of the life.

35. Thus also is the heart or light of God always generated in the body of this world, and that generated heart is *one heart* with the eternal, unbeginning, infinite heart of God, which is in and above all heavens.

36. It is *not* generated in and from the stars *only*, but in the *whole* body of this world; but the stars always kindle the body of this world, that the birth or geniture may subsist everywhere.

But here thou must well observe this.

37. The light or the heart of God taketh *not* its original barely from the wild rough stars, where, indeed, love and wrath are in each other, but out of or from the *seat* where the meek water of life is continually generated.

38. For that water, at or in the kindling of the wrath, was not apprehended by *death*, but subsisteth from eternity to eternity, and reacheth to all the ends and parts of or in this world, and is *the water of life*, which breaketh through death, out of which is built the new body of God in this world.

39. And it is *in* the stars, as well as in all ends, corners and places, but not in any place comprehensible or *palpable*, and it at once filleth or replenisheth all alike. It is also in the body of man, and he that thirsteth after this water, and *drinketh* thereof, *in him the light of life* *kindleth itself*, which is the heart of God; and there [in that place] presently springeth forth the Holy Ghost.

45. In this kindling of the light, in the stars and elements, the birth of nature did not thereupon *wholly transmute* or change itself into the holy meekness, as it was before the time of the wrath, *so that* the birth of nature be now altogether holy and *pure*: No, but it standeth in its sharpest, most austere, and most anxious birth, wherein the wrath of God *incessantly* springeth up like hellish fire.

48. The stars are only the kindling of the great house; for the whole house is benumbed in death, as the earth is; for the outermost birth or geniture is *dead* and benumbed, as the rind, shell or bark of a tree. But the astral birth is the *body* in which the life riseth up.

65. Now when thou beholdest the sun and stars, thou must *not* think that they are the *holy* and pure God, and thou must *not offer* to pray to them, or ask anything of them, for they are not the holy God, but are the kindled, *austere* birth or geniture of *his* body, wherein love and wrath *wrestle* the one with the other.

67. Now when thou worshippest or prayest to the *holy* God in his heaven, then thou worshippest or prayest to *him* in *that* heaven which is *in* thee, and that same God breaketh through in *thy* heart with his light; and in his light the Holy Ghost *breaketh* through, and generateth thy *soul* to be a new body of God, which ruleth and reigneth with God in *his* heaven.

68. For the earthly body which thou bearest is one body with the whole kindled body of this world, and thy body qualifieth, mixeth or uniteth with the whole body of this world; and there is no difference between the stars and the deep, as also between the earth and thy body; it is all one body. This is the only difference, thy body is a *son* of the whole, and is in itself as the whole being itself is.

The Twenty-Fifth Chapter

OF THE WHOLE BODY OF THE STARS AND OF THEIR BIRTH OR GENITURE; THAT IS, THE WHOLE ASTROLOGY, OR THE WHOLE BODY OF THIS WORLD.

19. Now when thou beholdest the stars, and the deep, together with the earth, then thou seest with thy bodily eyes nothing else but the *old* body in the wrathful death; thou canst not see heaven with *thy bodily* eyes, for the blue or azure sphere which thou seest above is *not the heaven*, but is only the old body, which may be justly called *the corrupted nature.*

21. But how deep or how large the place of this world is, *no man* knoweth, though some physicists or astrologers *have* undertaken to measure the deep with their measures of circles; their measuring is but conjectural, or a measuring of somewhat that is *comprehensible* or palpable; as if a man would grasp the wind in his fist.

22. But the true heaven is everywhere all over, to this very time, and till the Last Judgment Day; and the wrath-house of hell and of death is also in this world *everywhere*, even to the Last Judgment Day.

23. But the dwelling of the devils is *now* from the moon to the earth, and in the earth, in the deep caves and holes thereof; especially in wildernesses and desert places, and where the earth is full of stones and bitterness.

26. The whole body of this world is as a man's body, for it is surrounded in its utmost circle with the stars and risen powers of *nature*; and in that body the *seven* spirits of nature govern, and the heart of nature standeth in the midst or centre.

But here thou must observe exactly,
40. As far as the middle point or centre hath kindled itself, *just so* big is the *sun*; for the *sun* is nothing else but a kindled *point* in the body of nature.

41. Thou must not think that there is any other power or virtue in it, or belonging to it, than there is in the whole deep of the *body* everywhere, all over.

42. For should the love of God, through its heaven, kindle the whole body of this world *through the heat*, it would be everywhere all over as light as it now is in the sun.

49. But seeing the doors of the deep, and the gates of wrath, and the *chambers* of death also, are, through the love of God, set open *in my* spirit, *therefore* the spirit must needs look through them.

50. Accordingly I find, that the birth or geniture of nature standeth to this day, and generateth itself, just so as it did when it first took its beginning; and *whatsoever riseth* up in this world, whether men, beasts, trees, herbs, grass, mineral ores, or be it what it will, all riseth up in such a *quality*, manner and form as it first did; also every life, be it good or bad, taketh its original thus [as it did from the beginning].

51. For this is the *right* or law of the Deity: that every life in the body of God should generate itself in *one* manner or uniform way; though it be done through many *various* imagings, yet the *life hath* one uniform way and original in all.

55. Thou must not conceive it so, as if *my old* man were a *living saint* or angel. *No*, Friend, he sitteth with all men in the house of wrath and of death, and is a *constant* enemy to God, and sticketh in his sins, wickedness and malice, as all men do, and is full of faults, defects and *infirmities*.

56. But thou must know this, that he sticketh in a continual, *anxious* birth or geniture, but would fain be rid of the wrath and wickedness, and *yet cannot*. For he is as the whole house of this world, wherein love and wrath always wrestle the one with the other, and the new body always generateth itself in the midst or centre of the *anguish*. For so it must be, if thou wilt be born anew, otherwise no man *can reach* the regeneration.

Understand it aright.
68. The place where the SUN is, is such a place as you may choose or suppose *anywhere* above the earth; and if God should kindle the light by the heat, the *whole* world would be such a mere SUN; for that same power wherein the *sun* standeth *is everywhere* all over; and *before* the time of wrath it was everywhere all over in the place of *this world* as light as the *sun* now is, but not *so* intolerable.

The Twenty-Sixth Chapter

OF THE PLANET SATURNUS

Now observe:
55. When thou mindest, thinkest and considerest what there is in this world, and what there is without, besides or distinct from this world,

or what the essence of all beings is, then thou speculatest, contemplatest, meditatest in the whole body of God, who is the essence of all beings; and that is a beginningless, *infinite* being.

56. But it hath in its own seat no mobility, rationality or comprehensibility, but is a *dark* deep, which hath neither beginning nor end. In the dark deep is neither thick nor thin, opaque nor transparent, but it is a dark chamber of death, where nothing is *perceived,* neither cold nor warmth, for it is the *end* of all things.

57. This, now, is the body of the deep, or the very real chamber of death.

58. But in this dark valley there are the *seven* spirits of God, which have neither beginning nor end, and the one is neither the first, second, third or last.

59. In these *seven* dominions or regimens the regimen divideth itself into *three* distinct beings, where the one is not without the other, nor can they be divided the one from the other. But those seven spirits do each of them generate one another, from eternity to eternity.

60. The *first* dominion or regimen standeth or consisteth in the body of all things, that is, in the whole deep, or the being or essence of all beings or essences, which hath, in all corners and places thereof, in itself the *seven* spirits in possession, or in propriety indivisibly, or irresistibly, for its proper own.

69. But as long as the heart of the Deity, which [heart] is the corporeity, hideth itself in the body of this world in the outermost birth, the corporeity is a dark house; all standeth in great anguish and needeth a light, which is the sun, to shine in the chamber of darkness, until the heart of God doth move itself again in the seven spirits of God in the house of this world, and kindle the seven spirits.

70. Then the *sun* and stars will return again to their first place, and will *pass away* in such a form or manner; for the Heart and Light of God will give light and shine again in the *corporeity,* that is, in the body of this world, and replenish or fill all.

Mysterium Magnum

or

An Exposition of the First Book of Moses
called GENESIS

TRANSLATED BY JOHN SPARROW

Author's Preface

10. Since then the great Mysteries, the beginning of and original of all things, do befall us by divine grace; that we are able (as through the ground of the soul) to understand the same in real knowledge, with the inspired word of the divine science, we will write down its ground (so far as it is permitted to us) in this book: for a Memorial to ourself, and for the exercise of divine knowledge to the Reader.

13. And how the whole time of this world is portrayed and modellized, as in a watch-work: how afterwards it should go in time: and what the inward spiritual world, and also the outward material world, is: also what the inward spiritual man, and then the external man of the essence of this world, is: how time and eternity are in one another, and how a man may understand all this.

The First Chapter

5. This threefold spirit is one only essence, and yet it is no essence, but the eternal understanding, an original of the something: and yet it is the eternal hiddenness (just as the understanding of man is not confined in time and place, but is its own comprehension and seat), and the egress of the spirit is the eternal original contemplation, viz. a lubet* of the spirit.

8. This is now the eye of the abyss, the eternal chaos, wherein all (whatsoever eternity and time hath) is contained; and it is called Counsel, Power, Wonder and Virtue. Its peculiar and proper name is called GOD, or JEOVA, or JEHOVAH, who is outside of all nature, without all beginnings of any essence, a working in himself, generating, finding, or perceiving himself; without any kind of source from any thing, or by any thing: He hath neither beginning nor end, he is immeasurable, no number can express his largeness, and greatness, he is deeper than any thought can reach; he is nowhere far from any thing, or nigh unto any thing; he is through all, and in all: his birth is everywhere, and without and besides him there is nothing else: he is time and eternity, byss** and abyss, and yet nothing comprehends him save the true understanding, which is God himself.

The Second Chapter

6. When I take up a stone or clod of earth and look upon it, then I see that which is above and that which is below, yea, [I see] the whole world therein; only, that in each thing one property happeneth to be the chief and most manifest; according to which it is named. All the other properties are jointly therein; only, in various diverse degrees and centres, and yet all the degrees and centres are but one only centre. There is but one only root whence all things proceed: it severizeth itself only in the compaction, where it is coagulated: its original is as a smoke or vaporous breath or exhalation from the Great

*Lubet: Possibly from the Latin "lubet" or "libet": It pleases, or is pleasant or agreeable to.
**Byss: In the philosophy of Boehme, the opposite of abyss or void.

Mystery of the expressed Word; which standeth in all places in the re-expressing, that is, in the re-breathing (or echoing forth), a likeness according to itself; an essence according to the spirit.

8. For, I say, the inward world is the heaven wherein God dwelleth; and the outward world is expressed out of the inward, and hath only another beginning than the inward, but yet out of the inward. It is expressed from the inward through the motion of the eternal speaking Word, and closed into a beginning and end.

10. Therefore there is nothing nigh unto or afar off from God; one world is in the other, and all are only one: But one is spiritual, the other corporeal, as soul and body are in each other; and also time and eternity are but one thing, yet in distinct or different beginnings. The spiritual world in the internal [Principle] hath an eternal beginning, and the outward a temporal; each hath its birth in itself. But the eternal speaking Word ruleth through and over all; yet it can neither be apprehended nor conceived, either by the spiritual or by the external world, that it should stand still; but it worketh from eternity to eternity, and its work is conceived. For it is the formed Word, and the working Word is its life, and is incomprehensible; for the Word is without all essence, as a bare understanding only, or as a power that bringeth itself into essence.

The Third Chapter

15. The anguish-source is thus to be understood: The astringent desire conceiveth itself, and draweth itself into itself, and maketh

itself full, hard and rough: now the attraction is an enemy of the
hardness. The hardness is retentive, the attraction is fugitive: the one
will into itself, and the other will out of itself; but since they cannot
sever and part asunder one from the other they remain in each other as
a rotating wheel: the one will ascend, the other descend.

17. The anguish maketh the sulphurous spirit, and the compunction
maketh the Mercury, viz. the work-master of nature: he is the life of
nature, and the astringent desire maketh the keen salt-spirit ; and yet
all three are only one; but they divide themselves into three forms,
which are called Sulphur, Mercurius and Sal: These three properties
do impress the free lubet into themselves, that it also giveth a material
essentiality, which is the oil of these three forms (viz. their life and
joy), which doth quench and soften their wrathfulness; and this no
rational man can deny. There is a salt, brimstone and oil in all things;
and the Mercurius, viz. the vital venom maketh the essence in all
things, and so the abyss bringeth itself into byss and nature.

21. First know this: That the divine understanding doth therefore
introduce itself into fire, that its eternal lubet might be majestical and
lustrous, for the divine understanding receiveth no source into itself,
it also needeth none to its own being, for the all needeth not the
something. The something is only the play of the all, wherewith the
all doth melodize and play; and, that the universal or all might be
manifest unto itself, it introduceth its will into properties. Thus we, as
a creature, will write of the properties, viz. of the manifested God,
how the all, viz. the abyssal, eternal understanding manifests itself.
22. Secondly, the abyssal and divine understanding doth therefore
introduce itself into an anxious fire-will and life, that its great love and
joy, which is called God, might be manifest; for if all were only one,
then the one would not be manifest unto itself; but by the manifestation the eternal good is known, and maketh a kingdom of joy; else, if
there were no anguish, then joy were not manifest unto itself; and

there would be but one only will, which would do continually one and the same thing. But if it introduceth itself into contrariety, then in the contest the lubet of joy becomes a desire and a love play to itself, in that it hath to work and act; to speak according to our human capacity.

23. The original of the eternal spiritual and natural fire is effected by an eternal conjunction or copulation, not each severally, but both jointly, viz. the divine fire, which is a love-flame, and (2) the natural fire, which is a torment and consuming source.

The Fourth Chapter

12. And here is the original of the eternal death or devoration; and in this devoration is the highest arcanum or secret, for the true essential lively spirit and understanding proceedeth out of this devoration, and maketh another beginning; for the first beginning is God's, who introduceth himself from the abyss into byss to his own contemplation. But this beginning, which proceedeth again out of the devoration, is a spiritual beginning, and maketh three worlds, namely, (1) The dark fire-world in heat and cold; a rawness, wholly austere, devoid of essence: (2) The other world is the spiritual, light or angelical world: (3) And the third hath its beginning with the beginning of time. When God moved both the inward worlds, he thence brought forth and created this outward visible world into a form of time.

The Fifth Chapter

7. That which is good and holy in the light of the powers, that, in the darkness, is anxious and adverse. The darkness is the greatest enmity of the light, and yet it is the cause that the light is manifest. For if there

were no black, then white could not be manifest to itself; and if there were no sorrow, then joy were also not manifest to itself.

10. In the darkness he is an angry zealous God, and in the fire-spirit a consuming fire, and in the light he is a merciful loving God, and in the power of the light he is especially, above all other properties, called God; and yet 'tis all only the manifested God, who manifesteth himself through the eternal nature in introduced [*i. e.* inducted] properties. Else, if I would say what God is in his depth, then I must say, he is outside of all nature and properties, viz. an understanding and original of all essences. The essences are his manifestation, and thereof alone we have ability to write; and not of the unmanifested God, who, without his manifestation, also were not known to himself.

The Sixth Chapter

1. We acknowledge that God in his own essence is no essence, but only the alone power or the understanding to the essence, viz. an unsearchable eternal will, wherein all things are couched; and the same is ALL, and yet is only ONE, but yet desireth to manifest itself, and introduce itself into a spiritual essence, which is effected in the power of the light, through the fire in the love-desire.

10. This outward world is as a smoke, or vaporous steam or exhalation of the fire-spirit and water-spirit, breathed forth both out of the holy world and then also out of the dark world; and therefore it is evil and good, and consists in love and anger; and is only as a smoke or misty exhalation; in reference to and respect of the spiritual world; and hath again introduced itself with its properties into forms of the powers, to a pregnatress; as is to be seen in the stars, elements and creatures, and likewise in the growing trees and herbs. It maketh in itself with its birth another principle or beginning; for the pregnatress of time is a model or platform of the eternal pregnatress; and time coucheth in eternity: and it is nothing else, but that the eternity, in its wonderful birth and manifestation in its powers and strength, doth thus behold itself, in a form or time.

The Seventh Chapter

14. The Father is called a holy God only in the Son, that is, in the power of the light in the divine kingdom of joy, viz. in the great meekness and love; for that is his proper manifestation, wherein he is called God. In the fire he is called an angry God; but in the light or love-fire he is called the holy God: and in the dark nature he is not called God.

18. These seven properties are to be found in all things; and he is void of understanding that denieth it. These seven properties make, in the internal world, the holy element, viz. the holy natural life and motion; but, in this external world, this one element severizeth itself into four manifest properties, viz. into four elements; and yet it is but one only; but it divides itself into four head-springs, viz. into fire, air, water, and earth.

19. From the fire ariseth the air; and from the air the water; and from the water the earth, or a substance that is earthy. And they are only the manifestation of the one internal element, and are, in respect to the internal, as an enkindled smoke or vapour. So also the whole astrum is nothing else but the outbreathed powers from the inward fiery dark and light world, from the Great Mind of divine manifestation, and is only a formed model or platform, wherein the Great Mind of divine manifestation beholds itself in a time, and playeth with itself.

The Eighth Chapter

7. They which are in the dark would bear the name (or the names) of the great anger of God, according to the properties of the eternal nature in the wrath; and they which are in the light bear the names of the holy God, viz. of the divine powers; and they which are in the creation of the wonders of the outward world bear the names of the manifested powers of the outward world, viz. of the planets, stars and four elements.

11. For as we men have dominions upon the earth, so likewise the superior hosts under the astrum have their dominions; so also the oily spirits in the element-air: the whole deep between the stars and the earth is inhabited, and not void and empty. Each dominion hath its own Principle: which seems somewhat ridiculous to us men, because we see them not with our eyes; not considering that our eyes are not of their essence and property, so that we are neither able to see nor perceive them; for we live not in their Principle, therefore we cannot see them.

13. Also, the spirits of the external world are not all external, but some are only inchoative, which take their original naturally in the spirit of the external world, and pass away through nature, and only their shadow remains, as of all other beasts upon the earth.

14. Whatsoever reacheth not the holy element and the eternal fire-world, that, is devoid of an eternal life; for it ariseth out of time. And that which proceedeth out of time is consumed and eaten up of time; except it hath an eternal in its temporal, that the eternal doth uphold the temporal.

25. But now he is only called a God according to his light in his love, and not according to the darkness, also not according to this outward world. Albeit he himself is ALL, yet we must consider the degrees, how one thing mutually proceeds from another. For I can neither say of heaven, nor of darkness, nor of this outward world, that they are God: none of them are God; but [they are] the expressed and formed Word of God, a mirror of the spirit which is called God; wherewith the spirit manifesteth itself, and playeth in its lubet to itself with this manifestation, as with its own essence which it hath made. And yet the essence is not sundered from the spirit of God; and yet also the essence comprehends not the Deity.

27. The power in the light is God's love-fire, and the power in the darkness is God's anger-fire; and yet it is but one only fire, but divided into two Principles, that the one might be manifest in the other. For the flame of anger is the manifestation of the great love: and in the darkness the light is made known, else it were not manifest to itself.

The Ninth Chapter

16. Therefore the children of darkness, and the children of this world also, are wiser than the children of the light, as the Scripture saith. Thou asketh, Why? [Because] they have the magical root of the original of all essences manifest in them: and [to have] this was even

the desire of Adam: However [it was] the devil [who] persuaded them that they should be wiser, and their eyes should be opened, and they should be as God himself.

The Tenth Chapter

5. The creation of the outward world is a manifestation of the inward spiritual Mystery, viz. of the centre of the eternal nature, with the holy element: and was brought forth by the eternal-speaking Word through the motion of the inward world as a spiration; which eternal-speaking Word hath expressed the essence out of the inward spiritual worlds; and yet there was no such essence in the speaking, but was only as a breath or vaporous exhalation in reference to the internal, breathed forth, both from the property of the dark world, and also of the light world: and therefore the outward essence of this world is good and evil.

7. For we are not to think that there is the like in heaven, viz. in the spiritual world. In the spiritual world there are only the properties of possibility; but not at all manifest in such a harsh property; but are as it were swallowed up; as the light swalloweth up the darkness, and yet the darkness doth really dwell in the light, but not apprehended.

13. But when the speaking eternal Word in love and anger, for his malicious iniquity's sake, did move itself in the properties, viz. in the essence wherein Lucifer sat, to cast this wicked guest out of his habitation into eternal darkness; then the essence was compacted: for God would not permit or allow that he should any longer have these manifested powers, wherein he was a prince; but created them into a coagulation, and spewed him out of them.

14. And in this impression or conjunction the powers, viz. the watery and oily properties, were compacted; not that Lucifer did compact or create them; but [they were compacted by] the speaking Word of God, which dwelt in the manifested powers and properties: the same took away the disobedient child's patrimony, and cast him out as a perjured wretch, out of his inheritance into an eternal prison, into the house of darkness and anger; wherein he desired to be master over the essence of God's love, and rule therein as a juggler and enchanter, and mix the holy with unholy, to act his juggling feats and proud pranks thereby.

15. And we see very clearly with quick-sighted eyes, that thus it is: for there is nothing in this world so evil but it hath a good in it: the good hath its rise originally out of the good or heavenly property, and the evil hath its descent from the property of the dark world; for both worlds, viz. light and darkness, are in each other as one.

The Eleventh Chapter

19. All things of this world have a twofold body, viz. an elemental, from the fire, air, water and earth; and a spiritual body from the astrum. And likewise a twofold spirit, viz. one astral, the other elemental.

20. Man only (among all the earthly creatures) hath a threefold body and spirit. For he hath also the internal spiritual world in him; which is likewise twofold, viz. light and darkness; and [this] also corporally and spiritually. This spirit is the soul; but this body is from the water of the holy element, which died in Adam, that is, disappeared as to his life, when the divine power departed from him, and would not dwell in the awakened vanity.

23. The sidereal body is the highest excepting the divine in man; the elemental body is only its servant or dwelling-house, as the four elements are only a body or habitation of the dominion of the stars.

The Fifteenth Chapter

13. Thus understand by the inward creating the true heavenly image, viz. a holy [spiritual] man out of all the properties of the angelical divine world. Understand the inward body for the one only element, whence the four were expressed; and understand the outward man for the outward world, with the stars and four elements, viz. fire, air, water and earth, and also for the outward tincture, which is linked with the inward in the holy expressed Word, and is only severed by a Principle; where also the inward putteth forth an external life out of itself. The inward is holy, and the outward [life or Principle] in the tincture were likewise holy, if the curse were not come into it by reason of the awakened vanity; yet if the vanity be severed by the tincture, then it is holy, and a paradise, which shall open itself at the end of this world.

18. And the soul, in its real life and understanding, consists in three kingdoms: the first is the eternal nature, viz. the potent might of eternity, the dark and fire-world, according to which God calleth himself a strong zealous angry God, and a consuming fire, in which Lucifer hath wholly diabolized himself.

19. The second is the holy light-world, where the eternal understanding hath displayed itself through the fire's-sharpness, in the light of the great fiery love-desire, and turned the wrathful dark-and-fiery property to a kingdom of joy; which is the true manifestation of the Deity; and it is called the holy heaven of the angelical delight and bliss.

20. The third kingdom or world is the outward astral and elemental kingdom, viz. the air, with its domineering constellations, wherein all the five outward constellations rule, viz. the superior, and the inferior of the four elements, out of which the five senses take their original, wherein the vegetable and reasonable life consisteth. This is the animal soul, which ruleth in all the creatures of this wold, so also in all the outward heavens or constellations, and in all the earth or essences of the outward world.

27. The whole man with body and soul is threefold; and yet but one only man. The body is out of a threefold essence; and the soul is out of a threefold property of the spirit. An example thereof you have in the fire, light and air: the fire hath another property than the light and air have. The fiery body is the eternal constellation, viz. the magical constellation, the Great Mystery, out of which the outward constellation was produced, and brought into a creatural being or creation.

The Sixteenth Chapter

10. As God playeth with the time of this outward world, so likewise the inward divine man should play with the outward in the manifested wonders of God in this world, and open the divine wisdom in all creatures, each according to its property; so likewise in the earth, in stones and metals, in which also there is a twofold essence, viz. one from the original of the dark fire-world, and one from the original of the holy light-world.

The Eighteenth Chapter

6. Every creature bringeth its clothing from its mother's body; but man cometh miserable, naked and bare, in deepest poverty, and un-ability; and is able to do nothing; and in his arrival to this world he is the poorest, miserablest, forlornest, and most shiftless creature amongst all kinds, which cannot at all help himself; which doth sufficiently shew unto us that he was not created of God unto this misery, but in his perfection, as all other creatures were; which [perfection] the first man fooled away [or lost] by false lust; whereupon God afterwards, in his sleep, did first figurize him in the outward Fiat to the natural life in man and woman, according to the property of all earthly creatures; and hung upon him the worms'-carcass, with the bestial members for propagation, of which the poor soul is to this day ashamed, that it must bear a bestial form on the body.

7. Two fixed and steadfast essences were in Adam, viz. the spiritual body from the love-essentiality of the inward heaven, which was God's temple; and the outward body, viz. the limus of the earth, which was the mansion and habitation of the inward spiritual body, which in no wise was manifest according to the vanity of the earth, for it was a limus*, an extract of the good part of the earth; which at the Last Judgment shall be severed in the earth from the vanity of the curse, and the corruption of the devil.

8. These two essences, viz. the inward heavenly, and the outward heavenly, were mutually espoused to each other, and formed into one body, wherein was the most holy tincture of the divine fire and light, viz. the great joyful love-desire, which did inflame the essence, so that both essences did very earnestly and ardently desire each other in the love-desire, and love one another: the inward loved the outward as its manifestation and sensation, and the outward loved the inward as its greatest sweetness and joyfulness, and its precious pearl and most beloved spouse and consort. And yet they were not two bodies, but only one; but of a twofold essence, viz. one inward, heavenly, holy; and one from the essence of time; which were espoused and betrothed to each other to an eternal [being].

9. And the magical impregnation [or conception] and birth did stand in this fiery love-desire, for the tincture penetrated through both essences, through the inward and outward, and did awaken (or stir up) the desire; and the desire was the Fiat, which the love-lubet [or

*Limus: Mud, slime.

imagination] took, and brought into a substance. Thus the likeness of the express image was formed in this substance, being a spiritual image according to the first. [Just] as the Fiat had conceived and formed the first image, viz. Adam, so also the likeness was conceived out of the first for propagation; and in this conception the magical birth was also forthwith (effected), where, in the birth, the spiritual body became eternal.

10. Understand, if it had been that Adam had stood in the trial, then the magical birth had been thus [effected]: not by a sundry peculiar issue from Adam's body, as now, but as the sun through-shineth the water, and rends or tears it not. Even so [in like manner] the spiritual body, viz. the birth, had been brought forth, and in its coming forth had become substantial, without pains, care and distress, in a great joyfulness and delight, in a manner as both seeds of man and woman do receive in their conjunction a pleasant aspect. Even so also the magical impregnation and birth, had been a virgin-like image, wholly perfect according to the first.

The Nineteenth Chapter

4. Even then he forthwith sank down into a swoon, into sleep, viz. into an unability, which signifieth the death: for the image of God, which is immutable, doth not sleep. Whatsoever is eternal hath no time in it; but by the sleep the time was manifest in man, for he slept in the angelical world, and awaked to the outward world.

The Twenty-Second Chapter

77. We have nothing in this world for our own propriety but a shirt, whereby we cover our shame before the angels of God, that our abomination may not appear naked; and that is our own, and nothing

else; the other is all common: Whosoever hath two coats, and sees that his brother hath none, the other coat is his brother's, as Christ teacheth us.

78. For we come naked into this world, and carry away scarce our shirt with us, which is the covering of our shame; the rest we possess either by necessity of office, or else out of covetousness, out of the Serpent's false desire. Every man should seek the profit and preservation of his neighbour, how he might serve and be helpful to him; as one branch of a tree giveth its power, essence and virtue to the other, and they grow and bear fruit in one desire. Even so we are all one tree in Adam.

The Twenty-Fifth Chapter

15. To the description whereof we need an angel's tongue, and yet we are understood well enough by our school-fellows. We have not written this for swine; for none but those only who have been by and at the marriage of the lamb do understand what kind of entire inward great joy and love-delight is therein; and how dearly the bride receiveth her bridegroom in his pure, clear and bright fire's-property; and how she gives him her love-kiss: unto others this is dumb.

18. For prince Lucifer, before the time of the created earth, sat in the heavenly ens* in the angelical world *in the place of this world,* wherein the ens of the earth was comprehended in the Fiat, and brought into a compaction; his false imagination had tainted the limus before the compaction: *it was the place of his hierarchies.* Now the outward body of man was taken out of the limus of the earth in the Verbum Fiat, and formed according to the property of the human life, which was in the

---

**Ens: Existence or being as an abstract concept.*

Word. The Word formed (by or through the Fiat) the ens or limus of the earth according to the form of the human soul-life which was in the Word; and seeing God had set himself, through his Word, to be judge against the false infection and desire of the devil, to judge him and his enkindled [wickedness which he had brought to] substance, the judicial sword was already in the limus of the earth whereof Adam was made.

27. Now saith reason, Wherefore did not God examine this ens afore, out of which he created the earth, and man out of the same earth, before he created the earth and man? Forsooth, dear reason, here thou hast hit the matter right; God's omnipotence and omniscience must serve thy turn, whereby thou art able to bring all things into God's will, as rational fancy dictates. Hearken, O reason, dost thou know whence the earth is generated? Thou sayest, through the Word, viz. in the Verbum Fiat, I say so too. Now, what was this Word? Here look upon the earth and the whole creation, and thou wilt see what the desire of the Word hath brought into being or essence out of the spiritual ens. Thou wilt everywhere see good, and evil, and find out God's love and anger.

28. The Word was a full spiration from the spiritual fire- and light-world, according to which God calleth himself a strong, jealous, angry God, as to the fire, and a merciful, loving God as to the light.

29. Now if God should have quelled the first Principle, viz. the fire-source, in the ens of the earth (out of which it was created), whence should the light have its might? Doth not the Father, viz. the fire-world, beget the Son, viz. the light-world? But now, seeing the Word in the fire-world was vehemently enkindled by God's motion to the creation, as we may see by the coagulation of the stones, (if we were not blocks, and had only calfish understandings), wherewith then should this fire, but especially the enkindled ens in the coagulation, be reduced and brought again into the light, into the equal tempera-ture and harmony? God's love alone must then do it.

The Twenty-Sixth Chapter

36. The holy is unto God a sweet savour to life, and the wicked a sweet savour to the death in his anger; all must enter into his glory, and praise him; one in the property of his anger, who must call the evil good; the other in the property of his love, who must call the good, good. For so it must be, that the difference of the good and evil, of the light and darkness, of the life and death, may be known; for if there were no death, then the life were not manifest to itself; and if there were no darkness, the light were not manifest to itself.

37. And therefore the eternal free will hath introduced itself into darkness, pain, and source; and so also through the darkness into the fire and light, even into a kingdom of joy; that so the Nothing might be known in the Something, and that it might have a sport in its contra-will, that the free will of the abyss might be manifest to itself in the byss, for without evil and good there could not be any byss [ground or foundation].

38. For the evil maketh pain and motion, and the good causeth essence and power; and yet both essences are only one essence, as fire and light are only one essence, also darkness and light are only one; but it severs itself into two mighty distinctions, and yet there is no sundry separation, for one dwelleth in the other, and yet doth not comprehend the other; the one doth deny the other, for the one is not the other.

The Twenty-Seventh Chapter

4. The soul's free will is as thin as a nothing; and though it be in its body indeed encompassed with the something, yet its amassed or conceived something is in a false distempered essence, by reason of the original of sin.

5. Now if the free will would approach to God with the desire, then it must depart out of its false something, and if it now doth so depart, then it is bare and impotent, for it is again in the first nothing: for if it will come to God, then it must die to its false selfhood, and forsake it; and if it forsakes the same, then it is barely and merely as a nothing, and so it cannot go, work, or move. If it will shew its might, then it must be in something, wherein it doth imaginate and form itself.

The Twenty-Ninth Chapter

1. The eternal divine understanding is a free will, not arisen either from any thing or by any thing; it is its own peculiar seat, and dwelleth only and alone in itself, un-apprehended of any thing; for beyond and without it is nothing, and that same NOTHING is only ONE; and yet it is also as a nothing to itself. It is one only will of the abyss, and it is neither near nor far off, neither high nor low; but it is ALL, and yet as a Nothing. For there is in itself no contemplation, sensation or perceivancy whereby it might find a likeness in itself.

2. Its finding is its own forth-proceeding, so that it beholdeth itself in the egress, for that which is proceeded forth is its eternal lubet, sensation, and perceivancy; and it is called the divine wisdom. Which wisdom the unsearchable abyssal will apprehendeth in itself to its centre of lubet, viz. to an eternal mind of the understanding; which understanding the free will formeth in itself to its own likeness, viz. to an eternal-speaking, living [working] word, which the free will doth speak or breathe forth out of the formed wisdom of the lubet.

63. For this was a seven-and-seventyfold Racha [or avengement] upon the word of the understanding in the human life; that out of one only tongue, out of only one speaking Word and vital Spirit, a seventy-and-sevenfold tongue (viz. a confusion of the understanding) should be made. Before, the understanding lay in one sound [voice or harmony], but now the Racha came into it, and confounded and shattered it into seventy-and-seven parts.

64. For the human wheel of the sound or understanding was turned round, and the ten forms of fire, wherein time and eternity doth consist, did open themselves in every form of nature; which was seven times ten, which makes seventy; whereto also belongeth the centre, with its seven unchangeable forms of the eternal nature; which is altogether seventy-and-seven parts.

65. And herein lieth the Grand Mystery. Dear brethren, if ye were not clothed with the garment of the contentious languages, then we would be bold to declare something more in this place unto you; but ye are yet all captivated in Babel, and are contenders about the spirit of the letter; and yet have no understanding of the same. Ye will also be doctors and learned masters [forsooth], but yet ye understand not your own mother-tongue: ye bite and devour one another about the husk of the word, wherein the living Word doth form and amass itself, and ye neither desire nor understand the living Word. Ye speak only out of seven and out of seventy-and-seven, and yet ye have the Word in one number, wherein the whole understanding is contained: ye have it moving upon your tongues, yet ye cannot comprehend it.

The Thirty-Second Chapter

15. God brought eight persons into the ark, and of the clean beasts seven and seven, the male and its female. The seven persons point at the seven properties of the natural life, that God will have children out of all the properties into his eternal ark. The eighth person was Noah, and in Noah was the Righteous One, that was the Covenant, out of which the kingdom of Christ should come; therein stood the ark of Noah. But the ark hath three stories, which are the three Principles in one only divine manifestation, for each property of the three hath its own peculiar heaven and certain choir in itself.

20. Moreover, God said to Noah, *For yet seven days, will I cause it to rain upon the earth forty days and forty nights; and every living substance which I have made will I destroy from off the face of the earth.* Wherefore did God say, *after seven days* the flood shall come? Why not presently, either sooner or later; why doth he set even *seven* days? In this the seven properties of nature are contained mystically, in which the Verbum Fiat had introduced itself into an ens, viz. into the formed Word; that is, into the creation of the world; in which creation the formed Word repented at the vanity of all creatures, and moved itself through the generatress of nature in the formed Word, to destroy the turba.*

The Fifty-Second Chapter

7. The soul is not changed into the Deity, viz. into [Lahai-roi] the fountain of the living and seeing, for it is the eternal and temporal nature's. But the Deity is not nature's, but the will to nature, and manifesteth itself through the soul's nature. As the fire manifesteth itself through the iron, where then the iron seems as if it were mere fire, and yet it keepeth its own nature, and the fire also its own, and the one doth only dwell in the other, and one is the manifestation of the other. The iron hath no power over the fire, only the fire giveth itself to the iron, and the iron giveth its ens to the fire, and so both are changed into one, and yet remain two essences: So likewise it is to be understood with the soul and the Deity.

Turba: Crowd or large group of people (Latin)

The Seventieth Chapter

60. Christ, according to the eternal Word of the Deity, eateth not of the substance of heaven, as a creature, but of the human faith and earnest prayer, and the souls of men praising God, are his food, which the eternal Word that became man eateth, as a part; which appertaineth to no man or any other creature, neither can they eat it. And when he eateth the faith and prayer, together with the praise of God, from our souls, then the human faith, together with the prayer and praising God, becomes substantial in the Word of power, and is of one and the same substance with the substance of the heavenly corporeity of Christ, all alike to the only body of Christ, God, and substance, viz. God, man, and substance, all one.

The First Table

Mysterium Pansophicum

or

A Fundamental Statement Concerning the Earthly and Heavenly Mystery

TRANSLATED BY JOHN ROLLESTON EARLE

The First Text

1. The unground is an eternal nothing, but makes an eternal beginning as a craving. For the nothing is a craving after something. But as there is nothing that can give anything, accordingly the craving itself is the giving of it, which yet also is a nothing, or merely a desirous seeking. And that is the eternal origin of Magic, which makes within itself where there is nothing; which makes something out of nothing, and that in itself only, though this craving is also a nothing, that is, merely a will. It has nothing, and there is nothing that can give it anything; neither has it any place where it can find or repose itself.

The Third Text

3. We recognize, therefore, the eternal Will-spirit as God, and the moving life of the craving as Nature. For there is nothing prior, and either is without beginning, and each is a cause of the other, and an eternal bond.

4. Thus the Will-spirit is an eternal knowing of the unground, and the life of the craving an eternal being [body] of the will.

211

The Fourth Text

6. But in this Word is a will, which desires to go out into a being. This will is the life of the original will, and proceeds out of the pregnation, as out of the mouth of the will, into the life of Magic, viz. into Nature; and reveals the non-understanding life of Magic, so that the same is a mysterium in which an understanding exists essentially, and thus obtains an essential spirit. There, every essence is an arcanum or a mysterium of an entire being, and is thus a comprehension as an unfathomable wonder of eternity; for many lives without number are generated, and yet all is together but one being.

9. And thus we apprehend what God and Nature is; how the one and the other is from eternity without any ground or beginning. For it is an everlasting beginning. It begins itself perpetually and from eternity to eternity, where there is no number; for it is the unground.

The Fifth Text

3. The spirit-life is an entire fulness of the nature-life, and yet is not laid hold of by the nature-life. They are two principles in a single origin, each having its mystery and its operation. The nature-life works unto fire, and the spirit-life unto the light of glory. By fire we understand the fierceness of the consuming of the essentiality of Nature; and by light the production of water, which deprives the fire of power, as is set forth in the *Forty Questions on the soul*.

The Sixth Text

1. When we consider and take cognizance of ourselves, we find the opposition of all essences, each being the loathing of the other, and enemy to the other.

3. And hence arises all the power of this world, that one rules over the other. And this was not in the beginning commanded or ordained by the highest good, but grew out of the *turba*. Afterward Nature acknowledged it as her own being, which was born from her, and gave it laws, to generate itself further in the framed government. Where then this birth has climbed to regal prerogative, and has moreover sought the abyss, as the One, till it is become monarchy or empire. And there it is climbing still, and will be one and not many. And though it be in many, yet will the first source, from which all is generated, rule over all, and will alone be a lord over all governments.

The Seventh Text

1. Now, seeing in the mystery of the Eternal Nature we have such an arcanum from which all creatures evil and good were generated and created, we recognize it to be a magical essence or substance, where one Magic has by desire awakened another and brought it into being, where everything has elevated itself and carried itself to the highest power. For the Spirit of God is not a maker in Nature, but a revealer and a seeker of the good.

The Eighth Text

4. Thus the Magician of multiplicity is a proud, arrogant, covetous, malignant devourer, and a spirit from the desiring plurality; and is a false god. He is not attached to the Free-will of Nature, which hath the might of wonders at its command, and he has no understanding in the Divine Mystery, for he cleaves not with his will to that Spirit. Else, if his will were turned towards Freedom, the Spirit of God would reveal his magical mystery, and his wonders and works would, with his will, stand in God.

The Ninth Text

1. Seeing then there are two Magics in one another, there are also two Magicians who lead them, viz. two spirits. One is God's Spirit, and the other the Reason-spirit, in which the devil ensconces himself. In God's Spirit is the love of unity. And man cannot better prove or try himself than by giving serious attention to what his desire and longing impel him: the same he hath for a leader, and its child he is. Nevertheless, he now has power to break and change that will; for he is magical and possesses the power.

2. But there must be real earnestness; for he must subdue the astral spirit which rules in him. To do this, a sober calm life is necessary, with continual abandonment to God's will. For, to subdue the astral influence, no wisdom nor art will avail; but sobriety of life, with continual withdrawal from the influxes. The elements continually introduce the astral craving into his will. Therefore it is not so easy a thing to become a child of God; it requires great labour, with much travail and suffering.

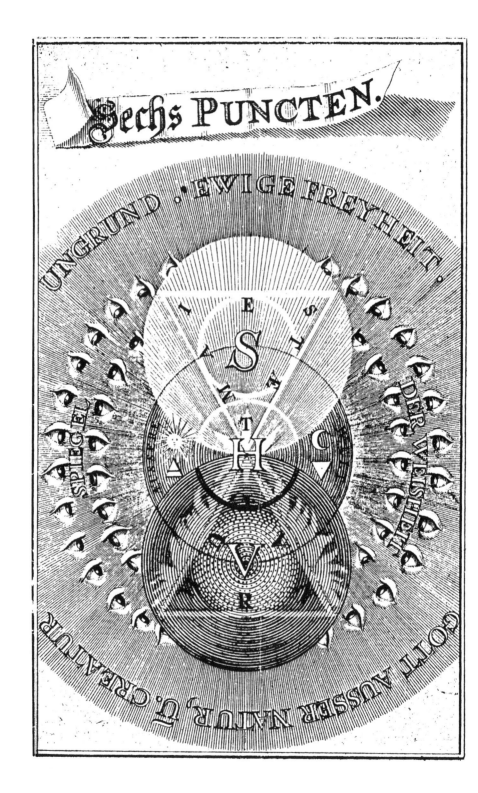

Sex Puncta Theosophica

or

High and Deep Grounding of Six Theosophic Points

TRANSLATED BY JOHN ROLLESTON EARLE

Chapter One

8. Thus we recognize the eternal Unground out of Nature to be like a mirror. For it is like an eye which sees, and yet conducts nothing in the seeing wherewith it sees; for seeing is without essence, although it is generated from essence, viz. from the essential life.

9. We are able then to recognize that the eternal Unground out of Nature is a will, like an eye wherein Nature is hidden; like a hidden fire that burns not, which exists and also exists not. It is not a spirit, but a form of spirit, like the reflection in the mirror. For all the form of a spirit is seen in the reflection or in the mirror, and yet there is nothing which the eye or mirror sees; but its seeing is in itself, for there is nothing before it that were deeper there. It is like a mirror which is a container of the aspect of Nature, and yet comprehends not Nature, as Nature comprehends not the form of the image in the mirror.

15. And herein we understand the eternal Essence of the triad of the Deity, with the unfathomable wisdom. For the eternal will, which comprehends the eye or the mirror, wherein lies the eternal seeing as its wisdom, is Father. And that which is eternally grasped in wisdom, the grasp comprehending a basis or centre in itself, passing out of the ungroundness into a ground, is Son or Heart; for it is the Word of life, or its essentiality, in which the will shines forth with lustre.

16. And the going within itself to the centre of the ground is Spirit; for it is the finder, who from eternity continually finds where there is nothing. It goes forth again from the centre of the ground, and seeks in the will. And then the mirror of the eye, viz. the Father's and Son's wisdom, becomes manifest; and wisdom stands accordingly before the Spirit of God, who in it manifests the Unground. For its virtue, wherein the colours of the wonders shine forth, is revealed from the Father of the eternal will through the centre of this Heart or Ground by the forthgoing Spirit.

19. Thus the essence of the Deity is everywhere in the deep of the unground, like as a wheel or eye, where the beginning hath always the end; and there is no place found for it, for it is itself the place of all beings and the fulness of all things, and yet is apprehended or seen by nothing. For it is an eye in itself, as Ezekiel the prophet saw this in a figure at the introduction of the spirit of his will into God, when his spiritual figure was introduced into the wisdom of God by the Spirit of God; there he attained the vision, and in no other way can that be.

20. We understand, then, that the divine Essence in threefoldness in the unground dwells in itself, but generates to itself a ground within itself, viz. the eternal word or heart, which is the centre or goal of rest in the Deity; though this is not to be understood as to being, but as to a threefold spirit, where each is the cause of the birth of the other.

21. And this threefold spirit is not measurable, divisible or fathomable; for there is no place found for it, and it is at the same time the unground of eternity, which gives birth to itself within itself in a ground. And no place or position can be conceived or found where the spirit of the tri-unity is not present, and in every being; but hidden to the being, dwelling in itself, as an essence that at once fills all and yet dwells not in being, but itself has a being in itself; as we are to reflect concerning the ground and unground, how the two are to be understood in reference to each other.

25. We are now to understand that the first Principle is magical in origin; for it is generated in desire, in the will. Hence its craving and contra-will to bring forth is also magical, namely to bring forth the second Principle.

26. And whereas in the first and second principle only a spirit without comprehensible [corporeal] being is understood; yet there is also the craving to give birth furthermore to the third Principle, wherein the spirit of the two principles might rest and manifest itself in similitude.

27. And though each principle has its centre, the first principle stands in magical quality, and its centre is fire, which cannot subsist without substance; therefore its hunger and desire is after substance.

41. But the first will, in which the gestation of Nature takes place, is deeper still than the centre of the word, for it arises from the eternal Unground or Nothing; and thus the centre of the heart is shut up in the midst, the first will of the Father labouring to the birth of fire.

42. Now, we are to understand that in the stern attraction a very unyielding substance and being is produced. And so then substance from eternity has its origin; for the drawing gives sting, and the drawn gives hardness, matter from nothing, a substance and essentiality. The sting of the drawing dwells now in this essentiality, pierces and breaks; and all this from the desiring will which draws.

43. And here we are to recognize two forms of Nature, viz. sour (astringent), that is Desire, and then the sting, which makes in the desire a breaking and piercing, whence feeling arises, that is, bitter, and is the second form of Nature, a cause and origin of the essences in Nature.

44. Now the first will is not satisfied with this, nor set at rest, but is brought thereby into a very great anguish; for it desires freedom in light, and yet, however, there is no brightness in freedom. Then it falls into terrible anguish, and so uplifts the desire for freedom, that the anguish, as a dying or sinking down through death, introduces its will into freedom out of the breaking, piercing and powerful attracting.

47. It is now clear what the first will to fire operates and effects, viz. stern, hard, bitter, and great anguish, which is the third form of Nature; for anguish is as the centre where life and will eternally take their rise. For the will would be free from the great anguish, and yet cannot. It would flee, and yet is held by the sourness (astringency); and the greater the will for flight becomes, the greater becomes the bitter sting of the essences and plurality.

48. It being unable then to flee or ascend, it turns as a wheel. And here the essences become mixed and the plurality of essences enters into a mixed will, which is rightly called the eternal mind, where plurality in numberless essences is comprised in a mind, where always from an essence a will again may arise according to the property of that essence, whence the eternal wonders spring.

49. Seeing then the great and strong mind of the form of anguish goes thus in itself as a wheel, and continually breaks the stern attraction, and by the sting brings into plurality of essences; but in anguish, in the wheel disposes again into a one, as into a mind: therefore now the anguishful life is born, viz. Nature, where there is a moving, driving, fleeing and holding, as also a feeling, tasting and hearing. And yet it is not a right life, but only a Nature-life without a principle. For it has no growth, but is like a frenzy or madness, where something goes whirling in itself as a wheel, where indeed there is a bond of life, but without understanding or knowledge; for it knows not itself.

Chapter Two

7. We find good and evil, and we find in all things the *centrum naturae* or the torture-chamber. But we find especially the spirit of the great world in two sources, viz. in heat and cold. Here, by cold we understand the centre of the sour sharp fierceness, and by heat the principle of fire, and yet they have but one origin from one another.

16. Reason says: God has made this world out of nothing. Answer: There was certainly for that no substance or matter that were outwardly palpable; but there was such a form in the eternal power in the will.

17. The creation of this world was brought about by an awakening of the Will-spirit. The inner will, which exists within itself, has stirred up its own nature, as the centre, which, passing out of itself, is desirous of the light which is pressing forth from the centre. Thus the centre has seized out of itself a being in desire; that is, it has seized or made for itself being in its own imagination in desire, and has also laid hold of the light's nature.

18. It has with the beginning laid hold of the Eternal; and therefore the beings of this world must enter by figure again into the Eternal, for they have been apprehended in the Eternal. But whatever was made or seized from the beginning in desire, that returns into its aether as into the nothing, merely into the mirror of imagination again. That is not of the Eternal, but is and belongs to the eternal Magic in desire. Like as a fire swallows up and consumes a substance whereof nothing remains, but becomes again as it was when as yet it was no substance.

19. And thus we give you to understand what this world's existence is. Nothing else than a coagulated smoke from the eternal aether, which thus has a fulfilment like the Eternal. It shuts itself in a *centrum* of a substance, and finally consumes itself again; and returns again into the eternal Magic, and is but for a while a wonder as a revelation of the Eternal, whereby the Eternal, which is manifest in itself, manifests itself also out of itself, and pours out its imagination; and thus renews that which was seized or made by the motion in desire, that the end may again enter into the beginning.

30. Thus is the Essence all in wrestling combat, that the wonders of the eternal world may become manifest in fragility, and that the eternal exemplar in the wisdom of God may be brought into figures. And that these models in the eternal Magic, in Mystery, may stand eternally to God's glory, and for the joy of angels and men; not indeed in being, but in Mystery, in Magic, as a shadow of being, that it may be eternally known what God has wrought, and what he can and is able to do.

32. We are now to consider the principles with their wonders. These are all three none else than the one God in his wonderful works, who has manifested himself by this world according to the property of his nature. And we are thus to understand a threefold Being, or three worlds in one another.

33. The first is the fire-world, which takes its rise from the *centrum naturae*, and Nature from the desiring will, which in eternal freedom has its origin in the unground, whereof we have not nor support any knowledge.

34. And the second is the light-world which dwells in freedom in the unground, out of Nature, but proceeds from the fire-world. It receives its life and sensibility from fire. It dwells in fire, and the fire apprehends it not. And this is the middle world.

35. Fire in the *centrum naturae* before its enkindling gives the dark world; but is in its enkindling in itself the world of light, when it separates into light and leaves the centre in darkness, for it is only a source in itself, and a cause of life.

37. The third world is the outer, in which we dwell by the outer body with the external works and beings. It was created from the dark world and also from the light-world, and therefore it is evil and good, terrible and lovely. Of this property Adam was not to eat, nor imaginate thereinto; but the three worlds were to stand in him in order, that one might not comprehend the other, as in God himself. For Adam was created from all the three worlds, an entire image and similitude of God.

39. Thus, if one see a right man, he may say: I see here three worlds standing, but not moving. For the outer world moves by the outer body, but the outer body has no power to move the light-world; it has only introduced itself into the world of light, whereby the light-world is become extinguished in man. He has, however, remained to be the dark world in himself; and the light-world stands in him immoveable, it is in him as it were hidden.

Chapter Three

3. That which in the dark world is a pang, is in the light-world a pleasing delight; and what in the dark is a stinging and enmity, is in the light an uplifting joy. And that which in the dark is a fear, terror and trembling, is in the light a shout of joy, a ringing forth and singing. And that could not be, if originally there were no such fervent, austere source.

4. The dark world is therefore the ground and origin of the light-world; and the terrible evil must be a cause of the good, and all is God's.

5. But the light world is only called God; and the principle between the light-world and the dark world is called God's anger and fierce wrath. If this be awakened, as by the devil and all wicked men, these are then abandoned of the Light and fall into the dark world.

6. The dark world is called death and hell, the abyss, a sting of death, despair, self-enmity and sorrowfulness; a life of malice and falsehood, in which the truth and the light is not seen and is not known. Therein dwell the devils and the damned souls; also the hellish worms, which the *Fiat* of death has figured in the motion of the omnipresent Lord.

Chapter Four

22. As also the inner man, who is from the Eternal and who goeth into the Eternal; he has only the two worlds in him. The property to which he turns himself, into that world is he introduced, and of that world's property will he eternally be, and enjoy the same; either a source of love from the light-world of gentleness, or a hostile source from the dark world.

Chapter Five

3. What the sun does in the third principle by transforming all hostile essence and quality into gentleness, that God's light does in the forms of the Eternal Nature.

4. It shines in them and also from them; that is, it kindles the forms of Nature, so that they all obtain the Light's will, and unite themselves and give themselves up wholly to the Light; that is, they sink down from their own essence and become as if they had no might in themselves, and desire only the Light's power and might. The Light accordingly takes their power and might into itself, and shines from this same power. And thus all the forms of Nature attain to the Light, and the Light together with Nature is but one will, and the Light remains lord.

Chapter Six

7. Reason says: Where are then the three worlds? It would have absolutely a separation, in which one were beyond or above the other. That, however, cannot possibly be, else the eternal unfathomable Essence were bound to sever itself. But how can that sever itself which is a nothing, which has no place, which is itself all? That cannot enter into particular existence which has no ground, which cannot be comprehended, which dwells in itself and possesses itself; but it proceeds out of itself, and manifests itself out of itself.

10. But the outer nature receives by the mirror the form of the spirit, as water does the lustre of the sun. We are not to think that the inner is far from the outer, like the body of the sun is from the water; though neither is that so, that the sun is far from the water, for the water has the sun's essence and property, else it would not catch the sun's lustre. Although the sun is a *corpus*, yet the sun is also in the water, but not manifest; the *corpus* makes the sun manifest in the water. And we are to know that the whole world would be nothing but sun, and the *locus* of the sun would be everywhere, if God was to kindle and manifest it; for every being in this world catches the sun's lustre. There is in all a mirror, that the power and form of the sun may be received in all that is animate and inanimate, in all the four elements and their essence and substance.

12. And thus then we are to recognize man. He is the inner and outer world (the cause, moreover, of the inner world in himself), and, so far as belongs to him, also the dark world. He is all three worlds; and if he

remain standing in co-ordination, so that he introduce not one world into the other, then he is God's likeness.

Chapter Seven

1. Every life is a clear gleam and mirror, and appears like a flash of a terrible aspect. But if this flash catch the light, it is transformed into gentleness and drops the terror, for then the terror unites itself to the light. And thus the light shines from the terrible flash; for the flash is the light's essence, it is its fire.

2. The flash contains the *centrum naturae*, being the fourth form of Nature where life rises, which in the steady fire, as in the principle, attains to perfection, but in the light is brought into another quality.

3. Now, the origin of the imagination [magical attraction] is in the first form of Nature, viz. in the desiring sourness, which carries its form through the dark world unto fire; for the first desire goes through all forms, makes also all the forms, and is carried as far as to fire. There is the dividing bound-mark of spirit, there it is born. It is now free. It may by its imagination go back again into its mother the dark world, or, going forward, sink down through the anguish of fire into death, and bud forth in the light. That depends on its choice. Where it yields up itself, there it must be; for its fire must have substance, that it may have something to feed upon.

18. The soul has in the time of the outer body three mirrors or eyes of all the three worlds. The mirror to which it turns itself, by that does it see. But it has no more than one as a natural right, namely the fire-flash, the fourth form of the dark world, where the two inward worlds separate (one into the darkness, the other into the light), and where its eternal origin is. The world into which the soul introduces its will, in the same it receives also substance, viz. a spiritual body. For this substance becomes for the soul's fire a food, or matter of its burning.

36. As love buds out of death (where the spirit of the will yields up itself to the fire of God, and sinks down as it were in death, but buds forth in God's kingdom with a friendly desire always to do well); so hath the will of wickedness given itself to perdition, viz. to wrathful, stern, eternal death, but buds forth with its twig in this corrupt world in outer nature, and bears such fruit.

37. By this should every one learn to know himself, he need only search for his distinctive property. To whatever his will constantly drives him, in that kingdom does he stand; and he is not a man as he accounts himself and pretends to be, but a creature of the dark world, viz. a greedy hound, a proud bird, a lustful animal, a fierce serpent, an envious toad full of poison. All these properties spring in him, and are his wood from which his fire burns. When the outer wood, or the substance of four elements, abandons him at his death, then the inner poisonous evil quality alone remains.

Chapter Eight

31. We are therefore highly to consider our life, what we would do and be at. We have evil and good in us. The one wherein we draw our will, its essence becomes active in us; and such a property we draw also from without into us. We have the two Mysteries, the divine and the devilish in us, of the two eternal worlds, and also of the outer world. What we make of ourselves, that we are; what we awaken in ourselves, that is moving in us. If we lead ourselves to good, then God's Spirit helps us; but if we lead ourselves to evil, then God's wrath and anger helps us. Whatever we will, of that property we obtain a leader, and thereinto we lead ourselves. It is not God's will that we perish, but his wrath's and our own will.

And thus we understand the fifth point. How a life perishes, and how out of good an evil comes, and out of evil a good, when the will turns round.

Sex Puncta Mystica
or
A Short Explanation of Six Mystical Points

TRANSLATED BY JOHN ROLLESTON EARLE

ON THE ELECTION OF GRACE. ON GOOD AND EVIL

1. God is from eternity alone all. His essence divides itself into three eternal distinctions. One is the fire-world, the second the dark world, and the third the light-world. And yet they are but one essence, one in another; but one is not the other.

2. The three distinctions are alike eternal and without bounds, and confined in no time nor place. Each distinction shuts itself in itself in a being; and its qualification is in accordance with its property, and in its qualification is also its desire, as the *centrum naturae*.

7. Human life is the hinge between light and darkness; to whichever it give itself up, in that same does it burn. If it give itself to the desire of essence, it burns in anguish, in the fire of darkness.

8. But if it give itself to a nothing, then it is desireless, and falls unto the fire of light, and then it cannot burn in any pain; for it brings into its fire no substance from which a fire could burn. Seeing then there is no pain in it, neither can the life receive any pain, for there is none in it; it has fallen unto the first *Magia*, which is God in his triad.

9. When the life is born, it has all the three worlds in it. The world to which it unites itself, by that it is held, and in that fire enkindled.

ON MAGIC. WHAT MAGIC IS. WHAT THE MAGICAL GROUND IS.

1. Magic is the mother of eternity, of the being of all beings; for it creates itself, and is understood in desire.

2. It is in itself nothing but a will, and this will is the great mystery of all wonders and secrets, but brings itself by the imagination of the desireful hunger into being.

3. It is the original state of Nature. Its desire makes an imagination (*Einbildung*), and imagination or figuration is only the will of desire. But desire makes in the will such a being as the will in itself is.

4. True Magic is not a being, but the desiring spirit of the being. It is a matrix without substance, but manifests itself in the substantial being.

5. Magic is spirit, and being is its body; and yet the two are but one, as body and soul is but one person.

6. Magic is the greatest secrecy, for it is above Nature, and makes Nature after the form of its will. It is the mystery of the Ternary, viz. it is in desire the will striving towards the heart of God.

7. It is the formative power in the eternal wisdom, as a desire in the Ternary, in which the eternal wonder of the Ternary desires to manifest itself in co-operation with Nature. It is the desire which introduces itself into the dark Nature, and through Nature into fire, and through fire, through death or fierceness into the light of Majesty.

8. It is not Majesty, but the desire in Majesty. It is the desire of the divine power, not the power itself, but the hunger or craving in the power. It is not God's Almightiness, but the directrix in God's power and might. The heart of God is the power, and the Holy Spirit is the revelation of power.

9. It is, however, the desire not only in the power, but also in the conducting spirit; for it has in it the *Fiat*. What the Will-spirit reveals in it, that it brings into a being by the sourness which is the *Fiat*; all according to the model of the will. According as the will makes a model in wisdom, so does desiring Magic receive it; for it has in its property imagination as a longing.

10. Imagination is gentle and soft, and resembles water. But Desire is harsh and dry, like a hunger; it makes the soft hard, and is found in all things, for it is the greatest thing (*Wesen*) in the Deity. It leads the bottomless to foundation, and the nothing into something.

11. In Magic are all forms of Being of all beings. It is a mother in all three worlds, and makes each thing after the model of that thing's will. It is not the understanding, but it is a creatrix according to the understanding, and lends itself to good or to evil.

17. Magic is the mother from which Nature comes, and the understanding is the mother coming from Nature. Magic leads into a fierce fire, and the understanding leads its own mother, Magic, out of the fierce fire into its own fire.

18. For the understanding is the fire of power, and Magic the burning fire; and yet it is not to be understood as fire, but the power or mother to fire. Fire is called the principle, and Magic is called desire.

ON MYSTERY. WHAT IT IS.

2. For *Mysterium magnum* is nothing else than the hiddenness of the Deity, together with the Being of all beings, from which one mysterium proceeds after another, and each mysterium is the mirror and model of the other. And it is the great wonder of eternity, wherein all is included, and from eternity has been seen in the mirror of wisdom. And nothing comes to pass that has not from eternity been known in the mirror of wisdom.

Profiles

BASARAB NICOLESCU is a physicist at the Laboratoire de Physique Théorique des Particules Élementaires of the Université Pierre et Marie Curie in Paris. He is also the author of *Nous, la particule et le monde* (Éditions Le Mail, 1985).

ROB BAKER is co-editor of PARABOLA, The Magazine of Myth and Tradition, for which he has translated material by Basarab Nicolescu, Amadou Hampâté-Bâ, and Marguerite Yourcenar.

JOSCELYN GODWIN is Professor of Music at Colgate University in New York and is the author of *Music, Mysticism and Magic; Robert Fludd; Mystery Religions of the Ancient World* and (most recently) *The Mystery of the Seven Vowels* (Phanes Press).

ANTOINE FAIVRE is Professor of the History of Esoteric and Mystical Traditions at the Sorbonne in Paris and also teaches at the University of Rouen and the University of California (Berkeley).

Illustrations

Typeset in Goudy and Goudy Handtooled

Design by James Sarfati and Kathy Massaro

Production Assistance: John Condon and Daniella Dooling

Printed by Thomson-Shore, Inc., Dexter, MI

All editions of PARABOLA BOOKS have sewn bindings
and are printed on acid-free paper.